TROMMER'S
WHITE LABEL BEER
(Bottle) .40

THE

ORIGINAL

F. W. I. L.

Lundy

Bros.

WELCOMES

YOU

TO

SHEEPSHEAD

BAY

HEINEKEN'S

IMPORTED

HOLLAND BEER

(Bottle) .60

...uors

WINES

	½ Bot.	Bot.
	4.25	8.00
	4.25	8.00

	Glass	½ Bot.	Bot.
	.60	4.25	8.00
	.60	2.75	4.75
	.60	2.75	4.75
	.60	2.25	4.00
	.55	2.75	4.75
	.60		4.00
	.50	2.75	4.75
	.45		3.50
	.45		4.00
	.60		4.00
	.45	2.25	4.00
	.55		4.00
	.90		
	1.00		

		2.75	5.00
45		2.75	5.00
			3.00

COGNAC-BRANDY

	Pony	Drink
Jack		.55
y★★★	.60	.80
r★★	.60	.80
artin	.60	.80
s.★★★★★	.60	.80
r	.60	.80

LIQUEURS

	.80	1.00
ing	.80	1.00
	.80	1.00
	.55	.80
	.80	1.00
	.80	1.00
	.80	1.00
	.80	1.00
Cordials	.50	.65
Cordials	.65	.90
s 10¢ extra		

...NKS

Flip	1.00
Cobbler	.70
bler	.70
monade	.65
ne & Seltzer	.65
g Nogg	1.00
	.90
ndy	1.00
	.90
	.75
ll	.90
ch	1.00
	.70
	.80
	.70

OCEAN and EMMONS AVENUES in SHEEPSHEAD BAY, N. Y.

Phones — Nightingale 6-9879 — 9286

Open All Year

Daily from 11 A.M. to 1 A.M. and on Saturdays 'till 2 A.M.

No connection with any other restaurant

WE CAN NOT BE RESPONSIBLE FOR PERSONAL PROPERTY UNLESS CHECKED

.15
.30
.60

.25
.60
.00
.50
.60
1.00
1.50
1.50

1.50
1.50
1.50
1.50
1.50

1.75

.50
.50
.80

1.50
1.50
1.50
1.50
1.50
1.60

2.00

1.75
2.50
1.00

.50

.45
.40
.45
.45
.40
.40

.60
.60
.60
.50

ream .40
75

.15
.15
.25
onade .... Split .15
.15

ESS CHECKED
DESK

DE

priced accordingly

SCHLITZ
RHEINGOLD
.40
.40
HT TO SERVE ALL LIQUOR CONSUMED ON THE PREMISES

BEER, ALE and STOUT
Bottle   HARP IRISH BEER
.40   BASS ALE
.40   GUINNESS STOUT
TROMMER'S WHITE LABEL BEER
HEINEKEN'S HOLLAND BEER

Bottle
.60
.60
.40
.40
.60

19367

Lundy's

Lundy's

REMINISCENCES AND
RECIPES FROM
BROOKLYN'S LEGENDARY
RESTAURANT

Robert Cornfield
*with recipes and
food notes by*
Kathy Gunst

■ HarperCollins*Publishers*

HarperCollins books may be purchased for educational, business, or sales promotional use. For information please write: Special Markets Department, HarperCollins Publishers, Inc., 10 East 53rd Street, New York, NY 10022.

FIRST EDITION

Designed by Joseph Rutt

Library of Congress Cataloging-in-Publication Data

Cornfield, Robert.
    Lundy's : reminiscences and recipes from Brooklyn's legendary restaurant / Robert Cornfield, with recipes and food notes by Kathy Gunst.
        p.   cm.
    Includes bibliographical references and index.
    ISBN 0-06-018741-7
    1. Cookery (Seafood) 2. Lundy's (Restaurant)—History. I. Gunst, Kathy. II. Title.
TX747.C74   1998
641.5'09747'23—dc21   97-35343

98 99 00 01 02 ❖/RRD 10 9 8 7 6 5 4 3 2 1

Contents

CONTENTS

VI

List of Illustrations

Prefatory Note

The Lundy's story is more than that of a beloved seafood restaurant. *Lundy's* is about the family that created and managed it, the neighborhood and borough it is part of, and most of all the patrons who thought it the best reason to live in Brooklyn. It is about Brooklyn pride and Brooklyn character.

Through trial and error we have tried to re-create the biscuits and chowder, and we offer other recipes associated with Lundy's old and new. In addition to creating a cookbook, we want to recall the story of a neighborhood, of the unique Irving Lundy, to find the reasons a restaurant haunts the memories of so many, and to suggest how its fortunes are tied to Brooklynites, who are continually coming and going and who maintain the borough's vitality and singular importance.

I grew up in Sheepshead Bay and it is the Lundy's of the late forties through the fifties that became an indelible part of my early years. In those years I could take bike trips down dirt paths through thickets of overgrown grass that began on the eastern side of Nostrand Avenue to the concrete stanchions of the long-departed Sheepshead Bay Speedway. Those remnants were as romantic and redolent of a lost civilization to me then as the fallen Greek temple columns of Sicily would be later. In part, then, this book is a journey to the places of my childhood and an attempt to recover their past and meaning.

—Robert Cornfield

Introduction

For over five decades Lundy's Restaurant of Sheepshead Bay was Brooklyn's most significant and celebrated restaurant. There were older restaurants and ones with considerable fame, but Lundy's was as quintessential a Brooklyn phenomenon as Ebbets Field. Because of its status for its patrons, Lundy's reflects and embodies much of the history of New York City and the borough of Brooklyn.

It is remarkable how many local Brooklyn institutions and how much history has been celebrated in books: so many remember Brooklyn of the twenties through the early sixties as a golden age, a glorious and rich period that one was privileged to have been part of. The Brooklyn Dodgers now have a shelf of books devoted to their story. There are books on Coney Island, the trolleys; memoirs by Larry King of Bensonhurst, Jerry Della Femina of Gravesend, Beverly Sills of Sea Gate; cookbooks devoted to Brooklyn specialties; histories; guidebooks; photograph albums. Its high schools—Erasmus, Midwood, James Madison, Lincoln—have national reputations and must have the best-attended reunions in the universe. And then there is the Brooklyn Bridge, whose importance, aside from its design, seems to reside in the fact that it connected Brooklyn with the rest of America, completing a national mission.

How does Lundy's restaurant—called an emporium, a palace, a castle, the largest restaurant in the world—figure in all this? There are many reasons. The history of its location, for one. In the nineteenth century, the southern shores of Brooklyn were a balmy boat trip from the congested streets of Manhattan. The excursion boat would travel down through the Narrows to the far marshes and beaches of lower Brooklyn, docking in a number of places: Bay Ridge, Bath Beach, Coney Island, and Brighton Beach. Well-to-do Manhattanites spent their summers in Brooklyn shore cottages or hotels. In his autobiography, Henry James tells of summering as a small boy at the commodious family hotel, the Hamilton House, named for the nearby fort in what is now Bay Ridge.

Sheepshead Bay's history was shaped by that of its neighboring sections: Coney Island, Brighton Beach, Manhattan Beach—traditional pleasure spots since the mid-nineteenth century and the locus of America's most celebrated amusement parks before Orlando, splendid beaches, great hotels, three grand racetracks when racing was this country's premier sport. Much of this had disappeared by 1934 when Frederick William Irving Lundy moved his Lundy Brothers' restaurant from an extended wooden pier on the bay of Sheepshead across the way to a full city block, but the memory of those grand days was there and so was the tradition of dining in style by the sea.

Sheepshead Bay's splendor was fairly tattered by the late twenties, but the city, encouraged by local real estate developers and community organizations, was determined to bring order to the shambles of docks and to beautify the area with well-paved streets and promenades. Its rehabilitation became in the early thirties a public works project, and the restaurant that most reaped the benefits of this civic effort was Lundy's. Lundy's move in 1934 from the bay pier to the site on the newly widened Emmons Avenue and the restaurant's reopening in late 1995 were part of similar area renewal strategies. The recent rebirth of Lundy's was as much of a spark as it was a reflection of the area's revitalization: the houses and streets of nearby

Midwood, Bay Ridge, and Manhattan Beach seem to have a new, reassuring gleam.

The interior of the 1934 Lundy's was cavernous, offering monumentality to the dining experience, and its stuccoed exterior was reminiscent of the luxurious resorts of California, Florida, and Long Island. Lundy worked with an architectural firm, but the design in all its detail was his own—he knew exactly what he wanted—and he brilliantly and precisely anticipated what would dazzle and please his patrons. For thousands of these patrons Lundy's was "their" restaurant—they called the waiters by name and the waiters knew their names, they had a favorite table, the parking lot attendant was a family friend—and real insiders knew someone who had dealings with Mr. Lundy, could recite how much money the place took in, and were privy to behind-the-scenes scandals. They felt they owned a piece of it—and they felt there was no better deal and no better lobster in the world. From the thirties through the fifties patrons would put on their best clothes when going to Lundy's. Dad wore a dark suit, tie, and fedora; Mom pinned on her small hat and fastened a fur piece with small pointy snout and beady eyes around the collar of her coat. The boys had their two-toned sport jackets—plaid front panels on brown backgrounds—and clipped on a bow tie; the girls had their spring jackets with gold buttons, belted in the back, over navy pleated skirts, their ensembles completed by Mary Janes. The special-occasion outfits made the lobster bib a necessity.

The most obvious appeal of Lundy's were the generous portions of fresh food—lobsters, clams, and oysters; chicken; oversized slabs of steak; distinctive biscuits; huge, fruit-filled pies. For many first- and second-generation Americans this was a distinctively American cuisine, and that distinctive American tone was what they sought when they moved to the newly developed "suburbs" of eastern and southern Brooklyn. In the twenties, first-generation Americans had moved from the Lower East Side and Brownsville tenements of their childhood to the new suburbia of southern Brooklyn, into grand apartment houses on Bedford and Ocean Avenues, and along the parkways of Ocean and Eastern, into two-story brick-clad houses on narrow tree-lined side streets. For many of the diners of the thirties and forties grand-scale restaurant eating was a new and sometimes intimidating luxury. Many local residents never ate out at all. Jerry Della Femina, who has written of his childhood in Gravesend, which borders Sheepshead Bay, reminds us of the intimidating atmosphere of restaurants: "We didn't go to restaurants, because we thought we'd be made fun of. Maybe we wouldn't be able to read the menu and the waiter would laugh at us."

While maintaining the integrity of their heritage in ethnically restricted—both voluntarily and involuntarily—neighborhoods, they yearned to participate in the bounty of the American dream, and food was a means of expressing assimilation and confirming the sense of being a member of a large community. Lundy's became *the* place for a Saturday night date, a Sunday family meal, a birthday or graduation celebration, the introduction to shucked-before-your-very-eyes clams and oysters, huge lobsters, or steamers dredged in butter. So different from the meats and stews of Irish food, German wursts, Italian spaghetti and meatballs, and the smoked meats, soups, knishes, puddings, and pierogi of Eastern European Jewish cooking, seafood was as unusual as Chinese food—not what you had at home, not what you were used to, and another sign of the variety and possibility of American life.

The meaning and success of Lundy's is due to a potent mix of food, a neighborhood with reminiscent ties to a turn-of-the-century luxury vacation site, a new population, a startlingly grandiose, evocative architecture, and a sublime bayfront location, a short distance from the beaches of Coney, Brighton, and Manhattan, and near the ferry to Rockaway Point.

A Lundy's meal was an indelible experience: the memory of those times is treasured as a time of rare community, exuberance, and largesse—plenty of food, of friends, of clatter, of the bustle and promise of life.

PART

1

The

Story

of

Lundy's

1

Prelude to Lundy's: Manhattan Beach and the Great Hotels

In the mid-nineteenth century, the section of southern Brooklyn that we know today as Sheepshead Bay was called the Cove, the eastern end of the Gravesend area that was home to a sparse farming community with a small contingent of fisherman. It was an area also popular with duck and snipe hunters. All that changed rapidly with the development of the island across a shallow, narrow inlet—the island called Coney. Coney Island was named for the rabbits that seemed to be its original inhabitants and comprises what we now recognize as three disparate entities: its western end, the Coney Island proper; its middle range, Brighton Beach; and its eastern end,

The Oriental Hotel and boardwalk, Manhattan Beach, 1880s. Kingsborough Community College now occupies this site, and the one remaining remnant of the hotel is a bandshell. Photograph by George Hall. © Collection of The New York Historical Society.

Manhattan Beach, the last to be developed. Each has its own character, and their pasts inform the present. At the turn of the century there was also another distinction made between what was called West Brighton—the entertainment site of amusement rides, beer halls, and restaurants—and at that time the least reputable area, the western end, now the gated community of Sea Gate.

Coney Island was always raffish, of a mixed character, where vice and simple pleasures commingled; Brighton was in the late nineteenth century the site of large middle-class hotels and a racetrack; and Manhattan Beach was first developed as a watering hole for the rich. In a subtle way these distinctions hold today, and when you cross Ocean Parkway from Coney to Brighton, or cross Coney Island

Avenue from Brighton to Manhattan Beach, you still move from one world to another: from gargantuan high-rises and projects shadowing a depleted amusement area to an enclave of Russian émigrés to a polyglot mix of, among others, newly established Asian-Americans, Hasidim, and old-timers. Depending on where you turn the corner, you will find store signs in English, Russian, Arabic, or Hebrew.

Before 1823, the island could be reached only on foot by crossing a creek when the tide was out, but in that year a toll causeway was constructed by the Coney Island Bridge and Road Company along the route of what is now Ocean Parkway. In 1849, another road was built to the island, its route roughly what is today McDonald Avenue. Ocean Parkway, once called the finest drive in America,

The Manhattan Beach Hotel, Manhattan Beach, 1880s. Today, this is the site of the Manhattan Beach bathing area. Photograph by George Hall. © Collection of The New York Historical Society.

running from Prospect Park to the Atlantic Ocean, was completed in 1876. In the same year, Ocean Avenue was marked out with the ultimate intention at its southern end of either bridging or filling in the Bay of Sheepshead to extend the road to Manhattan Beach.

In the 1840s, though Sheepshead Bay had inns and small hotels—Tappen's, which was a noted bay restaurant until it closed in 1948, opened as a carriage house serving clam chowder in 1842—the explosive transformation of a poor, thinly populated fishing village into a nationally celebrated resort begins with the story of Manhattan Beach and a real estate developer named Austin Corbin. He claimed that it was in 1873 when he vacationed on the eastern beaches of Coney, so his ailing child could reap the benefits of the sea air, that he envisioned an exclusive resort along the lines of his native Newport, Rhode Island. What resulted were two extravagant hotels, the Manhattan Beach and the Oriental, the latter constructed by the Long Island Rail Road. The Oriental was the more select, for it had no dining facilities for day visitors. A promotional brochure published in the mid-1880s, *The Story of Manhattan Beach*, tells how Corbin decided upon Manhattan Beach for his luxurious hostelries. He "perceived that in ignored, ill reputed Coney Island were all the requisites of a most desirable sea-side resort. He saw that with the elimination of the old class of visitors and the introduction of suitable accommodations for a better class, the island might take the place intended for it by nature." As part of his effort to ensure that there would be what he termed a better class, Corbin made certain that his hotels were restricted. The "objectionable" were excluded: "consequently, at no watering place is the representation of the best social classes larger than at Manhattan Beach." This was probably a knowing slap in the face to the less exclusive hotels of the Jersey shore.

On the way to Manhattan Beach from Sheepshead Bay, circa 1910. Originally built by developer Austin Corbin, the bridge was thought to be a temporary expedient for a roadway, never built, that would cross from the bay to Manhattan Beach at Ocean Avenue. Collection of The Brooklyn Historical Association.

7

The nearby Coney Island proper belonged to the hoi polloi. The anonymous author of *The Story of Manhattan Beach* recalls how distasteful the trip to Coney was:

> The writer distinctly remembers a visit paid by him to the island some seven years ago. The sail down the bay was made in an antiquated steamer. At the landing there was a barn-like dining room, with a still more barn-like bar-room attached, chops, steaks and chowder, of a very inferior quality, were purveyed at the prices of fashionable city restaurants, and, if in addition to refreshments the visitor desired a

D. Olagner's Ocean View Hotel, circa 1905. Less extravagant than the Manhattan Beach hotels, this bayside hotel had a commanding view of the Narrows. Photograph by George Hall. © Collection of The New York Historical Society.

bath, he was directed to a dilapidated shanty, where twenty-five cents were charged for a bathing suit, and a similar sum for the deposit of his purse or watch. At the end of a vacuous day the visitor returned to the city, lucky if he escaped robbery or insult, and he did not usually repeat his visit.

Corbin formed the New York and Manhattan Beach Railway Company in 1876 to service future hotel visitors and built the railway, originating at the southern end of Prospect Park, that took travelers to Manhattan Beach and determined the layout of Coney Island Avenue. The track beds supplied the base for the tracks of the Coney Island trolley line. It was Corbin who built the wooden bridge over the bay, joining Manhattan Beach and Sheepshead Bay. It serves the same purpose today. That bridge became a causeway of contention between the local community and Corbin, as he tried to tear it down to restrict access to Manhattan Beach.

The opening of the Manhattan Beach Hotel on May 4, 1877, was presided over by President Ulysses S. Grant, and the Oriental opened in 1880. The dining room at the Manhattan Beach offered the best to be had: "The table is spread with snowy linen and sparkling with crystal ware; the garçon is civilized and intelligent. What shall we order? Some grapes or peaches to begin with, certainly; then some half-shell clams with a bottle of Chablis; then a filet of sole, sauce tartare, or, do you not like smelts, breaded with dry toast and a cup of fragrant Mocha."

Ocean View Hotel Garden, circa 1905. Photograph by George Hall. © Collection of The New York Historical Society.

Just before the turn of the century a young newspaperman, Theodore Dreiser, newly arrived from the Midwest, and his brother, the composer Paul Dresser, who altered the family name—"My Gal Sal" was his most famous composition—spent a day at Manhattan Beach. From Long Island City they boarded a train that wound through meadows and marshes and "mucky lagoons" until they came to the sea.

In *The Color of a Great City*, a collection of his news reports, the American novelist recalls:

> And the beach, with its great hotels, held and contained all summer long all that was best and most leisurely and pleasure-loving in New York's great middle class of that day. There were, as I knew all the time, other and more exclusive or worse beaches, such as those at Newport and Coney Island, but this was one which served a world which was plainly between the two, a world of politicians and merchants, and dramatic and commercial life generally. I never saw so many prosperous-looking people in one place, more with better and smarter clothes, even though they were a little showy. . . . It was no trouble for any one of those most famous on Broadway and in the commercial and political worlds. They swarmed here.

What enticed many of the hotels' visitors to the area were the great racetracks across the bay. By far the most prestigious track was the Sheepshead Bay Racetrack, built in the early 1880s by the Coney Island Jockey Club, whose governors included August Belmont, William K. Vanderbilt, H. Newbold Morris, F. Augustus Schermerhorn, Leonard Jerome, and H. P. Whitney. The other tracks were the Brighton Beach Race Course, which William A. Engeman had established in 1879, and the Gravesend Racetrack, built by the Brooklyn Jockey Club and which featured the Preakness

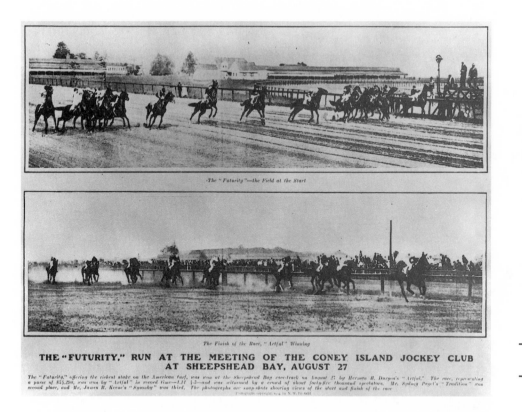

The "Futurity"—the Field at the Start

The Finish of the Race, "Artful" Winning

THE "FUTURITY," RUN AT THE MEETING OF THE CONEY ISLAND JOCKEY CLUB
AT SHEEPSHEAD BAY, AUGUST 27

The "Futurity," offering the richest stake on the American turf, was run at the Sheepshead Bay race-track on August 27 by Herman B. Duryea's "Artful." The race, representing a purse of $55,250, was won by "Artful" in record time—1.11 4/5—and was witnessed by a crowd of about forty-five thousand spectators. Mr. Sydney Paget's "Tradition" won second place, and Mr. James R. Keene's "Sysonby" was third. The photographs are snap-shots showing views of the start and finish of the race.

The Futurity at the Coney Island Jockey Club (Sheepshead Bay Racetrack), circa 1904. Collection of The Brooklyn Historical Association.

and the Brooklyn Handicap. The latter was located between Ocean Parkway and Gravesend Avenue, and Kings Highway and Avenue U. For thirty years, the area was the racing capital of the world. The track season ran from May 15 through October 15, and the three tracks scheduled their major events so as not to conflict. The spring season opened with the Brooklyn Handicap at the Gravesend track, and then the spectators moved on to the Suburban at Brighton, and then finally to the Futurity, which was run at the Sheepshead Bay Racetrack in early September. In 1910, the Futurity moved to

THE "FUTURITY" AT SHEEPSHEAD BAY, AUGUST 31

12

Saratoga and finally to the Aqueduct in 1916.

The presence of this great racing hub determined who would be the new occupants of Sheepshead Bay and the surrounding region. Trackhands and jockeys from the South moved to the area, creating strong Irish-American and African-American communities. To the east and along the shore (now the Plum Beach section), Alanson Treadwell, head of the noted department store Treadwell, Jarman & Slote, began development of Lincoln Beach by buying up property and building grand houses. The prospects of the Rockaways and the ocean beyond, and Manhattan Beach to the southwest made this a splendid location, and by the end of the century the shore was lined with a dozen mansions, some occupied by Brooklyn's great brewers. What is today the Sheepshead Bay Yacht Club is the former home of Julius Liebmann, one of the original owners of Rheingold Beer. The strip became known as Millionaires' Row.

Hotels and restaurants flourished with names that still resonate: a former chef of Tappen's opened his own restaurant, Villepigue's (the family name continues on billboards as an advertising leasing firm around New York City), the Jerome Hotel and Restaurant, the Lewis House, Hotel Beau Rivage, the Nelly Bly Hotel, Sheirr's

Restaurant, Seidels's and Schuessler's, the United States Hotel, the Bayside Hotel and the Atlantic Hotel (a section of which still exists appended to Lundy's). Longtime residents who live in converted summer bungalows originally built in the early years of this century (to be found around both sides of Emmons, just three or four blocks east and west of Nostrand Avenue) have schooled themselves in the area's history and can show you the sites. Tappen's and Villepigue's are most often cited as the place of the first Shore Dinner, served to Diamond Jim Brady. The terrifying number of courses included eight lobsters, two portions of scallops, one portion of mussels, fried shrimp, steamed clams, scungilli, bluefish, flounder, and trout. In the book *Sodom by the Sea*, the author names the then-famous who

Bay View Hotel, 1912. This hotel was on the northwest corner of Emmons Avenue and Sheepshead Bay Road. Courtesy of Ron Schweiger.

made Sheepshead Bay the Hamptons of its day: "Many of the race-track followers patronized Villepigue's. Whitneys and Vanderbilts drove down in tallyhos that mingled with the tandems, barouches and phaetons of Harry K. Thaw, William A. Brady, Grace George, Fanny Ward, Nora Bayes, Edward Gold, Clarence Mackey, Maurice Barrymore and his theatrical discovery Marie Dressler." Dressler was discovered at Coney Island, while appearing in a carnie show. And the neighborhood gave rise to another celebrity. Billie Burke, Florenz Ziegfeld's widow but best remembered as the good witch in the film of *The Wizard of Oz*, was born in Sheepshead Bay.

But the glory was not to last. In the late teens, and after an absence of many years, Theodore Dreiser returned to Manhattan Beach:

> Of that old, sweet, fair summery life not a trace. Gone were the great hotels, the wall, the flowers, the parklike nature of the scene. In twenty-five years the beautiful circular pavilion had fallen into the sea and a part of the grounds of the great Manhattan Hotel had been eaten away by winter storms. The Jersey Coast, Connecticut, Atlantic City, aided by the automobile, had superseded and effaced all this. Even the great Oriental, hanging on for a few years and struggling to accommodate itself to new conditions, had at last been torn down.

However, the final blow had not been dealt by the automobile or other resorts: the area's strongest raison d'être had been the racetracks, but declining attendance forced the Brighton track closed in 1907, and in 1910 in a reforming crusade to rid the state of lawlessness, Governor Charles Evans Hughes, who had just trounced William Randolph Hearst in the gubernatorial race, outlawed race-

Villepigue's Inn, corner of Ocean Avenue and Voorhies Avenue. A favorite restaurant of Diamond Jim Brady and Lillian Russell, where, legend has it, the Shore Dinner was born. Tappen's would move from its original site on Emmons Avenue to this building in the midforties. Collection of Ron Schweiger.

15

track gambling. The best reason for track attendance disappeared and the great Sheepshead Bay track shut down. Probably the investors were just looking for a chance to move on to other sites, for the hotels of the area had lost their panache and exclusivity as well. After the Manhattan Beach Hotel was torn down in 1911, modest summer bungalows were built on a portion of its grounds.

After serving for a brief time as an aerodrome, the abandoned, empty track was refashioned to accommodate another mode of transportation: from racing horses to racing cars. In 1915 Harry S. Harkness and associates built a $3.5 million speedway on the site of the Sheepshead Bay Racetrack. It was advertised as the fastest automobile track in the world, and the most celebrated drivers of the new sport appeared there, notably Barney Oldfield and Nick DiPalma.

But car racing did not attract the same crowd as the horses had: it didn't have the prestige or the kind of season that made an excuse for social events. The smaller hotels and some restaurants went the way of their grand Manhattan Beach neighbors. When in 1918 the Jerome Hotel at Shore Road and Emmons was torn down, the *Brooklyn Daily Eagle* commented that "Sheepshead Bay has gone to the dogs since racing stopped." Obviously, they were not impressed by auto races.

The interior of Villepigue's Inn, circa 1910. Collection of The Brooklyn Historical Society.

By 1922, Emmons Avenue was considered a local, smelly disgrace. The *Brooklyn Daily Eagle* reported that the waterfront area of Sheepshead Bay was "completely occupied by business activities conducted in dilapidated shacks, or from narrow and flimsy wharf structures extending out over the mud into deep water. At the same time this conglomeration of shacks is an important market for fish, clams, lobsters, and other seafood, and the base of a fleet of more than 1000 fishing boats, yachts, and other small craft." Local fish included cod, pollock, blackfish, sea bass, porgies, mackerel, fluke, flounder. There was a call for a major rehabilitation effort, which focused on the piers and shanties of Emmons Avenue. The first task would be the construction of the new bulkheads and the deepening of the bay. The fishing fleet had inadequate berthing space, and certain landings were simply inaccessible at low tide. In addition, low tide brought with it odors that were considered a menace to health, for the sewers at the end of Ocean Avenue dumped directly into the bay. The bulkhead job was eventually completed in the mid-1930s as a project of the Brooklyn work relief program which involved fifteen thousand men at a cost of $17 million.

There was additional impetus for this renewal, and that was the development of the land just to the north. The First World War had caused a halt to all construction, and the immediate postwar years were ones of a calamitous housing scarcity combined with unbridled rent gouging. To correct this, the state and city established rent stabilization boards and encouraged real estate development by means of tax relief incentives. In 1923–24 a syndicate formed by Joseph F. Day acquired from Harry Harkness the property collectively known as the Sheepshead Bay–Harkness Estate, which included the former raceway. The syndicate then began to both sell off and develop the property. At the first auction four thousand lots were sold, and came

Sheepshead Bay at low tide, circa 1905. The bay was first a small fishing and farming community before becoming a notable resort. Photograph by George Hall. © Collection of The New York Historical Society.

to a total of $2.5 million, out of which the syndicate made a profit of $1 million. Grand houses that were occupied during the season by racehorse owners, actors, and bookmakers were destroyed. (A few of these elaborate summer cottages, though, can be found on the north side of the Belt Parkway, from Nostrand Avenue to Sheepshead Bay Road.)

In 1906 an investment group headed by George C. Austin fulfilled an ambition of Austin Corbin's to develop the property north of the Manhattan Beach hotels. The swampland was filled in and grand houses built on streets laid out with names, in honor of Corbin's heritage, sounding like a Shakespearean history battle roster: Exeter and Beaumont, Oxford and Norfolk, Langham and

Kensington. Later, Joseph Day took over the development of the whole of Manhattan Beach and it was he who built the Manhattan Beach Baths (on the site of the Oriental Hotel) and the Brighton Beach Bath and Club House. The area's housing boom was also encouraged by the extension of the subway and bus lines and the increased use of the automobile.

In her splendid book *Brooklyn! An Illustrated History*, Ellen Snyder-Grenier details what these real estate manipulations accomplished:

> Instead of stressing aesthetics and quality, real-estate promotional materials hawked new developments as "big" or "dynamic," calling Sheepshead Bay the "New Flatbush," perhaps a reference to Flatbush's recent phenomenal growth. By 1925, a thousand homes had been built (in 1922 and 1923 Brooklyn led the nation in housing construction). To keep profits high, developers built on large tracts using standardized designs and materials. Sellers emphasized houses equipped with driveways and garages and interiors designed for "modern" living. Before long, the area's rural character had changed.

The population and building boom of the twenties, coupled with the redevelopment of Sheepshead Bay, provided young Irving Lundy with the great opportunity of his life, and he didn't miss his chance.

19

2

F. W. I. L. Himself

It was in the early years of the nineteenth century that the first Frederick Lundy arrived in Brooklyn. A 1902 history of a distinguished Pennsylvania Quaker family named Lundy—not related to the Brooklyn Lundys—devotes a section to other families who shared the name. The discussion of the Brooklyn family provides a clue to its origins. "Frederick Lundy, a lad of fourteen years, was brought to Long Island, N.Y., from Bremen Haven, Germany, in 1838, by the Nostrand family. Frederick had lost both his parents when a child and had been reared by his grandmother. In after years he wrote several times to Bremen Haven and made inquiry about his ancestry, but he was unable to gain any information. He married and left a family; among his children were John, Charles, Jerome, Frederick Jr., and Walter. His sons under the firm name of Lundy Brothers now control the seafood market at Manhattan Beach, Long Island." Carol Lundy Bamert, a niece of Irving Lundy, told me that family history passed from generation to generation records that the

Rear view of the Atlantic Hotel, the site of the present-day Lundy's. East 19th Street between Emmons Avenue and Shore Road. Photograph by Eugene Armbruster. Collection of The Brooklyn Historical Association.

Lundys were Dutch with some English forebears, and since Brooklyn was originally a Dutch and English settlement, this destination would make sense for someone coming from Holland. Frederick II, Irving's father, was born March 26, 1862, and his wife, Athenaise Gladding, in 1871. Athenaise's father, William Gladding, was justice of the town of Gravesend.

The family enterprise of fish purveying was begun by the grandfather and great-uncles of the Irving Lundy who built the 1930s restaurant on Emmons and Ocean Avenues. It was the Lundy family business that supplied the fish for Corbin's great Manhattan

Corner of Emmons Avenue and East 19th Street, 1923. The building with the tower was the Atlantic Hotel, and it stands today, much altered, at the rear of Lundy Bros. Restaurant. Photograph by Eugene Armbruster. Collection of The Brooklyn Historical Association.

Beach hotels and others in the area, for by the early 1880s the Lundys were long established local fish sellers. In Henry R. Stiles's 1884 history of the city of Brooklyn, the Lundy brothers are prominently mentioned as leading citizens and businessmen. In 1883, the Lundy Brothers' fish store was located on Shore Road, as listed and advertised in *Overton's Coney Island and Sheepshead Bay Guide and Directory* of that year. There were also two other stores, one at West 8th Street in Coney Island and another at West 1st Street and Sheepshead Bay Road. Fred Lundy had a rowing, sailing, and fishing boat concession at the eastern end of the bay. By the turn of the century Lundy Brothers was renowned as among the city's largest fish and seafood purveyors.

The full name Frederick William Irving Lundy yielded the initials F.W.I.L. that emblazoned the restaurant, and the rest of its name, Lundy Brothers, carried forward the tradition of a family business and paid tribute to two of his younger brothers who had recently died.

Frederick William Irving Lundy—he preferred to be called Irving—was the eldest son of seven children: his brothers were Clayton, Stanley, and Allen, and his sisters were Athenaise (named after her mother), Gladys, and Elaine. Born in 1895 in a high and rambling house on Voorhies and East 23rd, Irving had the privileged childhood of the scion of a respected and socially prominent family.

McLoughlin's Casino and the Bayside Hotel, circa 1910. Emmons Avenue between Ocean Avenue and East 19th Street. Courtesy of Brian Merlis.

The plush sporting world and lively social scene was his turf, and his father, Frederick II, involved in local politics, knew the city's political nabobs and knew too the power that came from these connections. The most prominent and notorious local politician of the last quarter of the nineteenth century was kingpin John Y. McKane, and Frederick succeeded him in many posts and emulated his real estate manipulations. McKane was married to the daughter of the Nostrand family that had brought Frederick's father to America. Frederick emulated McKane's vision of local control through real estate holdings and influence peddling and both Frederick's and Mc Kane's social worlds consisted of fellow politicos.

That world of favors, real estate deals, and freewheeling entrepreneurship was not lost on Frederick's son Irving. Except for the Manhattan Beach, Oriental, and Brighton, McKane built all the hotels in the area and also controlled the gambling dens and brothels of Coney Island. This was made all the easier since he was county commissioner, chief of police, and the local Sunday school teacher, but, as a result of political reform movements in the early nineties, he began a five-year prison term for election fraud in 1893.

Frederick was a registrar of Kings County, and was elected alderman in 1900. In 1910 he succeeded Kenneth Sutherland as Democratic leader of the Sixteenth Assembly District, which encompassed Sheepshead Bay, Coney Island, Bath Beach, and Bensonhurst. But his political ambitions turned out to be costly and he declared bankruptcy in 1914. He died at age fifty-six on November 7, 1918, from diabetes. In addition to his children, he left two brothers, John and Charles, and a sister, Carrie Osborne. A year earlier his wife Athenaise had succumbed suddenly to influenza.

Young Irving had idolized his mother and had inherited her red hair, flushed complexion, and finely chiseled features. As he later con-

"New Flatbush." Advertisement for new homes and property, 1924. The area included the former site of the Sheepshead Bay Racetrack, Manhattan Beach, Marine Park, and lower Midwood. Collection of The Brooklyn Historical Association.

fessed to his employee Marion Anderson, he never fully recovered from the grief of her death. After serving in the navy in the First World War, Irving, as eldest son, took over the family fish business, which was now run from a frame building that extended over a pier at Ocean and Emmons Avenues. To the burden of early responsibility was added a family tragedy that invoked a lifelong sense of guilt and mortal vulnerability that haunted and ultimately overwhelmed his life.

In late January of 1920, just off Rockaway Point, near a tiny spot the family had claimed as Lundy's Island, a boat that held Irving's younger brothers Clayton, twenty-one, Allen, nineteen, and Stanley, eighteen, and a worker capsized in freezing water. Two reasons have been cited for their being in these waters at the time: they were either tending their clam beds or they were engaged in a most common Prohibition-era occupation—rum running. Clayton, Allen, and the worker clung to the overturned boat, but Stanley was thrown some distance and he struggled to swim back among the ice floes. Before he could reach them, he slipped under the water, and Clayton broke loose to rescue him. After diving under, Clayton brought up Stanley's seemingly lifeless body, but Stanley's weight, their heavy clothes, and the freezing water exhausted Clayton's strength, and the two brothers sunk out of sight and never resurfaced. Their bodies were found only after a two-week search. In reporting the incident, the *Brooklyn Daily Eagle* noted that the family lived together at 2120 Voorhies Avenue, and they were called oyster dealers.

Within three years, Irving and Allen and their sisters suffered the loss of both parents and two brothers. These tragedies tightened the bonds between the remaining family members. The baby of the family, Elaine, was raised by her sister Gladys and Gladys's husband George Higgins. The death by drowning of his brothers scarred Irving's life, branding him with a permanent fear of water and a premonition of impending violent death, which never left him though he lived into his early eighties. Another phobia was of sweets, for he believed he had inherited his father's disposition to diabetes. But this was not the end to devastating family catastrophes, for he would suffer in his late years another horrifying calamity.

In the early 1920s Irving began to secure his world by enlarging the fish business, indulging what would be a lifelong interest in acquiring property locally and on Long Island and in upstate New York, and securing his pier for some bootleg smuggling activity. The entire family was engaged in fending off with shotguns turf intruders interested in taking advantage of their landing. Any suspicious boat approaching in the night would first be shouted off and then given a warning barrage. Allen Lundy Jr. has said that his father, uncle, and aunts were a pretty tough bunch. As along all borders of the United States, the authorities were more than likely to wink at such activities, though there would be the occasional raid to still any criticism. With their own cutter, the family became skillful at avoiding the Coast Guard. The family oyster and clam beds in Jamaica Bay provided a good, reasonable screen, and Irving was hedging his bets with both shady and legitimate activities. The repeal of Prohibition didn't frighten him; by that time he knew full well how to make millions legitimately.

In the 1890s, those who had property along Emmons Avenue were granted riparian rights to build a waterfront pier into the bay. In 1910, Frederick's wife Athenaise purchased the lot across from the pier that Frederick was leasing for his fish store, and eventually Irving would buy from his brother and sisters their share of this property. This gave Irving more secure title to the pier on which the first restaurant was established.

Ten months after he bought Sheepshead Bay–Harkness Estate, Joseph Day was able to offer six hundred newly built buildings in the property. Collection of The Brooklyn Historical Society.

The F.W.I.L. Lundy Bros. Fish Shop and Dock, circa 1931. Courtesy of Brian Merlis.

In 1926, he opened with Allen the first F.W.I.L. Lundy Brothers restaurant on the fish store pier by extending the pier further into the bay on pilings. In these years Irving was very much the flashy bon vivant—he told Marion Anderson that among his pals of those years was Henry Ford. He indulged his taste for sharp clothes, expensive rings, and diamond stickpins, and he found a companion for late-night excursions to the expensive restaurants and speakeasies of Manhattan in the business's accountant, a weekend pilot and hunter, Henry Linker. The stocky, dashing Linker was to remain Irving's closest friend and associate for thirty years, and on weekends, Linker drove Lundy to Lundy's Catskill estate at Wawarsing, where Linker hunted and Irving oversaw the livestock. Janet Higgins, married to a nephew of Lundy, says that Linker left his wife for Irving. But Lundy often confided in friends about a showgirl girlfriend in the twenties who he continued to support for the rest of her life. He never married, he said, because he wanted no mother-in-law.

On October 18, 1926, Irving and Henry were abducted in front of Lundy's home at 625 Ocean Avenue (near Albemarle Road) by three men. In the scuffle, Irving took off his ring and with the heel of his shoe buried it in the dirt. The abductors drove the two of them to Maspeth, Long Island, in what the *Brooklyn Eagle* described as a seven-hour trip. While Irving was shut in a chicken coop, the men drove back to the restaurant with Linker, who was forced to open the safe, where they found $4,000 in cash. In the morning, after the kidnappers expressed their disappointment about how little they got but complimented Irving on his swell restaurant, the two men were let go and given from their own money the $9 cab fare back to Brooklyn. Lundy found the ring he had dropped in front of the house. Within days, two of the kidnappers, Conrad "the Bull" Bulto and James "Hot Air" McNulty, were caught and eventually given life sentences. What was confirmed for Irving was his vulnerability and the knowledge that someone was always out there trying to get him and his money. His fear of crowds grew and he no longer walked openly through his restaurant. Gradually, he withdrew from being seen in public and guarded his privacy. The restaurant's front man was Allen, and most often when patrons claimed they "knew" Mr. Lundy, it was the affable Allen Lundy they had met.

His restaurant and its management were a passion with Irving. When in the twenties the pier restaurant suffered a damaging fire, he had it repaired in one day. Though the dining room itself was forbid-

The dockside Lundy Bros. Restaurant from the bay, 1931. Courtesy of Brian Merlis.

Main entrance to the dockside Lundy Bros. Restaurant. Courtesy of Brian Merlis.

den territory for the now shy and nervous Irving, he did go into the kitchen to supervise the cooking—both Irving and Allen taught themselves to be skilled cooks and personally trained the staff.

Lundy was truculent and self-protective: in 1928 he sued the city because it had built a bridge to Far Rockaway in Jamaica Bay that, he claimed, ruined his twelve acres of clam beds. But a year before bridge construction had begun, the Board of Health had condemned the bay as polluted and had forbidden the cultivation of shellfish in the area. Lundy lost that suit. It wasn't in him to give in without a fight, and he was to win later battles with the city over condemnation rights and licensing. Lundy was a litigious person, and he had almost as many lawyers as lawsuits.

With the late 1920s Sheepshead Bay renewal project gearing up, the shanty businesses and restaurants of the bayside knew they were doomed. But this gave Lundy his opportunity to build what he conceived of as the largest restaurant in America. He knew where it would be—right across the street from the pier. The McMahan family, who had built and managed the Bayside Hotel and Casino since the 1880s, had announced as early as December 1924 that they planned to demolish the hotel, and they reportedly leased the property for $500,000. However, it wasn't until 1929 that Lundy secured the rights, which included the riparian rights, to this site on Emmons Avenue between Ocean Avenue and 19th Street. Condemnation proceedings for the bayside stores and restaurants began in 1930, but actual destruction didn't commence until early 1934. In the meantime, in 1932, Maurice W. Monheimer, Irving's lawyer of the moment, announced that Lundy's would establish a $600,000 restaurant on the north side of Emmons Avenue.

On April 16, 1934, the *Brooklyn Daily Eagle* was pleased to note that all the structures on the south side of Emmons Avenue had

31

The dockside Lundy Bros. Restaurant, from the bay, 1931. Courtesy of Brian Merlis.

been razed by laborers recruited from the ranks of the unemployed to facilitate the widening of the avenue. However, that wasn't entirely true. There was a holdout. Lundy refused to vacate the pier restaurant until the new one was finished, and so for a full six months, fighting off borough officials, he singularly held up the extension of Emmons Avenue. Finally, on October 15, 1934, the new restaurant was ready. Just as the last clam was shucked on the pier, the first one at the new Lundy's was pried open. Lundy wanted the move to be one of high drama and visibility. He called the newspapers to have them witness his waiters stationed in assembly-line fashion across Emmons Avenue, handing the old furnishings and equipment from the old place to the new.

On March 8, 1936, Justice Charles C. Lockwood awarded to Lundy Brothers restaurant $145,000 for the land and underwater property that was taken for the new docks and widening of the avenue. Lundy had asked for $436,714, but the award granted him was the largest given to any property owner. It was on record that the property on which the new restaurant stood had been sold in 1926 for a total of $375,000. For the pier and land on which the old restaurant had stood, all that was awarded was $20,000 (Lundy asked for $210,756). The *Brooklyn Daily Eagle* reported that "Nothing was allowed for the old wooden restaurant building that extended partly over the water, because in all these years, the court held, the riparian rights did not allow the property to be used for restaurant purposes."

3

The Restaurant and Its Architecture

When Lundy gave instructions to his architects, Block and Hess, for the design of his block-long restaurant, the particular architectural style he dictated must have been in his mind for some time. This style is usually described as Spanish Mission or Spanish Colonial Revival. Its hallmarks are exterior and interior stucco walls (intended as in Mediterranean countries and in Florida and California to deflect the heat of intense sun), raked red-tile roofs, and wrought-iron grillwork. It was a design particularly suited for resort areas and came to signify class, brilliant light, and spaciousness. Lundy had traveled in the West, knew Florida well, and so would have been familiar with its use for both luxury homes and commercial properties. For a Brooklyn restaurant of its day the design was unique—it signified a redefinition of Sheepshead Bay (in the early thirties the ambition of local developers was to make the bay "a modern Venice"), as did the clearing out of the dockside businesses and the widening of Emmons Avenue. Lundy could well have been influenced by the Spanish renaissance designs of the buildings that had been developed in the twenties on the southern shore of Long Island as the Gold Coast of New York in rivalry with Atlantic City and other Jersey shore resorts. This effort had been masterminded by the state senator and real estate magnate William J. Reynolds, who built the grand hotels of Long Island's Atlantic Beach in the pseudo-Spanish, pre–Art Deco style in emulation of Florida's Gold Coast. The scheme was an attempt, like Austin Corbin's in the 1880s, to appeal to folks newly rich in the prosperity of the twenties. The one

The Sheepshead Bay Pedestrian Bridge, 1933. In the background is the Bayside Hotel, future site of the new Lundy's. This was taken a year before the reconstruction of the docks would thoroughly alter the character of the area. Photograph by P. L. Speer. Collection of The New York Public Library.

remaining example is the 1928 Lido Beach Hotel, now a condominium, whose architects Schultze and Weaver had just designed the imperious new Waldorf Astoria on Park Avenue. Another example was the 1927 Half Moon Hotel in Coney Island.

Variants of the Spanish Mission style were used for some of the houses on elegant Ocean Parkway. Tiled roofs and stucco walls were also common to the mansions of Ocean Parkway, mansions that had been occupied by early movie stars—the Vitagraph movie studio on Avenue M was not very far away, and a 1910 version of *Ben Hur* had been filmed on Manhattan Beach—and also William K. Vanderbilt II's Eagles' Nest, now the Vanderbilt Museum, in Centerport, Long Island. In 1927 Vanderbilt remodeled the original 1910 mansion in the "Spanish" style: that mix of stucco surfaces,

The Pedestrian Bridge looking toward Shore Boulevard of Manhattan Beach, 1933. Photograph by P. L. Speer. Collection of The New York Public Library.

The Atlantic Hotel and the Casino, 1933. The sign indicates the location of the parking lot for the dockside Lundy Bros. Restaurant. By this date, Irving Lundy owned the property and was preparing to build his new restaurant here. Collection of The New York Public Library.

37

tiled roof, and wrought-iron grillwork throughout. It is likely that the Eagles' Nest's architecture was the primary influence for Irving Lundy's design of his restaurant. This was not the only Vanderbilt-Lundy connection. In the forties, Irving Lundy bought from Mrs. Alfred G. Vanderbilt the Elizabethan-style Samuel A. Salvage mansion, recently owned by Villa Banfi Importers, now in private hands. It is close to Eagles' Nest on Long Island, in Brookville, and it was a house he only visited but never slept in.

Offering an exotic vision of a sunlit Mediterranean climate, the Spanish Mission style implied class, and it was especially classy for a seafood restaurant, which were usually designed with a fish shack in

The east end of Sheepshead Bay was the site of a popular beach until the late thirties. Collection of The New York Public Library.

mind. It still is classy. Today, the neighborhood, shorn almost entirely of its historic buildings, is given architectural distinction by the tile roofing and arched doorways of Lundy's.

What was most startling about Lundy's was the broad expanse of the two-story beige stucco exterior. Since the grand hotels had vanished, this was instantly the largest building in the area. The design took shape during the construction, and the three active designers were Walter Hesse, Pietro Ghiani, and Irving Lundy, who would bring to the site each morning additional architectural drawings. Originally the restaurant accommodated 850 diners on the first floor and an equal number on the floor above.

The capping of its roof with the dark red tiles was a neighborhood event. Longtime Sheepshead Bay resident and neighborhood activist Margaret McCord remembers it as she does V-J Day. The neighbors stood in rows across the street, watching the progress of the roof tiling from early dawn. It was the first and only time in her more than sixty years in the bay that she caught a glimpse of Mr. Lundy. Someone in the crowd pointed him out, and she saw his face half covered by his fedora. He was hunched over, making himself as inconspicuous as possible.

It wasn't only the extent and color of the exterior that created a fantasy of luxury, but the evocative drama of the details. Lundy had ground clam shells mixed into the mortar for the interior stucco walls to make a more secure bond, but he was well aware of its symbolic significance. Maroon awnings led to the entranceways, the windows were

Overview of Sheepshead Bay, 1931. These docks, fish markets, tackle shops, and restaurants would be destroyed in 1934. Compare with pages 18 and 87. Photograph by Ernest Tanare. Collection of The Brooklyn Historical Association.

red and blue stained glass, encasing his personally designed coat of arms that featured his initials: F.W.I.L. Over the doorways were fish mosaics by local artisans. Because of these dramatic color contrasts, the restaurant always seemed spanking new, and Irving Lundy with his mania for cleanliness and upkeep made sure it stayed that way: the paint was specially mixed to his specifications, and both exterior and interior were maintained in pristine condition.

Lundy's new building, a huge rectangle filling the block, included a grand dining hall in two large sections on the first floor, enclosed and patio dining on the second floor, two kitchens, storage area below the extent of the upper restaurant, a liquor bar facing Emmons, a clam bar in a special extension of its own on Emmons

The old docks of Sheepshead Bay that were razed in 1934. The white building jutting out into the bay in the background (right) is the dockside Lundy Bros. Restaurant. Photograph by P. L. Speer. Collection of The New York Public Library.

The end of a day of fishing, on the docks of Sheepshead Bay. Photograph by P. L. Speer. Collection of The New York Public Library.

with roll-up windows, vast rest rooms reached by marble stairways with handcrafted wrought-iron railings, a lounge for the staff, an apartment for the owner, a room for suppliers. The large chimney was "originally treated as a bell tower with a tiled, gabled roof."

With its stained glass, carved wooden lintels and grilles, wrought-iron railings, and lamps and chandeliers, the restaurant gave off an aura of careful splendor. The New York Landmarks Preservation Commission report names the building's features that determine its architectural style. "The simplicity of the design, the limited number of materials, the restrained ornament, the contrasts of light and shade, and the treatment of the different portions of the building as individual blocks with separate roofs, identify Lundy's specifically as

Emmons Avenue between East 19th Street and Sheepshead Bay Road, 1934. To the right is the rebuilt Lundy's. Note that Emmons Avenue is being widened and repaved as part of a WPA project. Photograph by P. L. Speer. Collection of The New York Public Library.

an example of the vernacular version of [Spanish Colonial Revival] style."

The Bayside Hotel was demolished, except for a back extension that was kept and resurfaced to match the old building. This was called the Annex and held the business offices and lounges. It is a thrill for those interested in building construction of the past to see this building, a fragment from the nineteenth century, shorn now of its stucco exterior, still standing behind the landmarked Lundy building.

Originally, the second story was set back for open-air dining, and plantings cascaded over the balcony, but in the postwar boom years of the late forties this was enclosed to allow for year-round dining.

Today, arches that separate the main dining area from a short outer alcove indicate the original exterior wall of the second floor. In the sixties, Lundy was told that the second floor didn't conform to fire regulations. His response was characteristic; rather than conform to regulations, he closed it off to the public. In 1945, a brief one-story extension was added to the back of the Ocean Avenue side that was later called the Teresa Brewer Room in honor of the wife of a nephew of Lundy. This no longer exists.

The Brooklyn of the thirties and forties had neighborhoods of wonderful richness—as the Brooklyn of today still has to a splendid extent. Not far away from Sheepshead Bay were the grand houses and

The bay being drained and deepened during the construction of the new bulkheads, 1934. Collection of The New York Public Library.

From the Pedestrian Bridge, 1935. A panoramic view of Emmons Avenue, from Sheepshead Bay Road to Dooley Road (one block west of Bedford Avenue), with the rebuilt Lundy's dominating the landscape. Photographs by P. L. Speer. Collection of The New York Public Library.

broad streets of Fort Hamilton and Bay Ridge. In the late twenties and thirties the bungalows of Manhattan Beach that had been built on the grounds of the grand hotels were torn down and in their stead came substantial homes for the upper middle class. The grand Victorian houses of Flatbush represented Brooklyn at its most refined, and the new houses of Midwood, though less ambitious in size, were pleasing and attractive. There were shopping areas that

indicated domestic richness: the emporia of downtown Brooklyn, of course, but also along much of Flatbush Avenue as it cut through the entire length of the borough, and on a slightly smaller, local scale Kings Highway or Bay Ridge's 86th Street. Lundy's new restaurant, ambitious and extravagant in scope, was actually very much a part of the Brooklyn tradition of fine living. It was that spirit that encouraged the fantastic housing developments of the twenties.

4

The People Who Ate at Lundy's and a Waiter Who Served Them

Through the thirties to the fifties and even beyond, Canarsie, Gerritsen Beach, Flatlands, and Mill Basin were increasingly covered with new brick houses—in a row, semidetached, detached, with stoops, front and back porches, driveways, or garages—and new streets. And the people who moved to these houses were leaving behind the tenements of Williamsburg, Brownsville, Crown Heights, Bushwick, and East New York for the suburbs of outer Brooklyn.

The colonization of southern Brooklyn in these years was to be followed, beginning in the late forties, by a new mass movement to the
suburbs from Brooklyn to Long Island.

During the twenties, the Jewish population in Brooklyn
increased 700 percent, with huge settlements particularly in southern Flatbush, Midwood, and Sheepshead Bay and the Coney Island
neighborhoods. The builders for these new neighborhoods were often
Jewish. The new residents came from the Lower East Side and from
Brownsville. The construction of the entrances to the Williamsburg
and Manhattan Bridges—1903 and 1909 respectively—had devas-
tated the Lower East Side and pushed the evicted into Brooklyn.
Ben Halpern, in an essay entitled "America Is Different," states the
situation well: "The generation that entered the immigrant ghetto
was confronted by one overwhelming task: to get out, or to enable
the next generation to get out. This task they accomplished."
Neighborhoods such as Flatbush, which had previously been domi-
nated by middle-class Irish and white Protestants, became Jewish.
The Italians and the Jews of the early twentieth century were following the pattern of movement of earlier Irish and German immigrants. But with this movement there was no widespread integration:
greater ethnic isolation was the result. There were ethnic blocks
divided by streets. Gravesend west of Ocean Parkway became Italian,
and east of the parkway was Jewish. As Jerry Della Femina notes in
his autobiography, the neighborhoods were insular and xenophobic
and remarkably distinct in goals, lifestyles, and values.

For these newcomers, spacious apartments on boulevards like
Eastern Parkway or Ocean Parkway, far from the city, on tree-lined
streets, or small, typically two-story houses, with a basement and at
least a suggestion of a front yard, meant not only economic success,
but their entrance into the great American society. They were shed-

ding their immigrant status, losing their accents and old manners, and yet they did this in neighborhoods where they bundled with "their own." Not all of New York was open to second-generation immigrants: Park Slope and Brooklyn Heights barred Jews, as did Sea Gate at the western end of Coney Island, and some sections of Flatbush advertised themselves as "sensibly restricted," as did apartment complexes in Queens.

The new residents of the southern area of Brooklyn had made their money in the frenzied real estate market of the twenties, in city industries like clothing manufacturing, printing, contracting, and jewelry, and they valued education as the gateway to further success. For Jews their religion was redefined in relation to the new society: the growth of Conservative and Reform Judaism, the synagogue as social center, with gyms and conference rooms and banquet rooms. And there was a consequent exploration of new foods into the forbidden. Now there were three sets of plates: for dairy, for meat, for nonkosher. Then one might have kept kosher at home but chosen to eat nonkosher outside, or when at a nonkosher restaurant, avoided the notoriously nonkosher pig products and shellfish. This eating outside the rules was another way of being an American.

These upwardly mobile people were the Lundy's clientele. In a real sense, southern Brooklyn had developed a suburb within its own borders, and a trip to Lundy's by a trolley ride or a less-than-twenty-minute car ride was like a trip to a coastal resort restaurant. The resort feel of Lundy's made it a weekend destination for those from other boroughs—there was the abundance of the Shore Dinner, the walk around the bay and across the wooden bridge to the beautifully landscaped streets of Manhattan Beach, the overarching sky over the Narrows. The names Sheepshead Bay and Manhattan Beach were still imbued with a sense of the pleasure resorts of the past, though only a hairsbreadth away from Brighton Beach and Coney Island. Brooklyn was like a continent of tiny countries, with borders every two or three miles. It was given unity by certain landmarks: Ebbets Field, Prospect Park, movie palaces, the downtown shopping center, and its great seafood restaurant—the pride of Sheepshead Bay—Lundy's.

Memories of the past always involve food, but there is something special about the food of Brooklyn—the restaurants, the candy stores, the food served on holidays, the corner treats. It is as if these delicacies were the prime luxuries of the times. There is always the regret that what we had then is no longer. The best egg cream, made with Fox's U-Bet chocolate syrup, milk, and the right amount of seltzer, could be had only at the major trolley intersection of Nostrand and Flatbush Avenues. The expansion of the transit system with new subways, buses, and trolley routes made the whole borough and its neighborhood specialties accessible to all. Mrs. Stahl's baked potato knishes (the light dough a thin covering over the filling) were worth traveling the BMT to the Brighton Beach station—or were the glorious end to a day at the beach or Brighton Private, where you got a locker for the season. Or, for whatever reason, Nathan's frankfurters of Coney Island were the best—though some claimed the prize for Shifrin's Hebrew National. A friend surmised that it was the aroma of the sea air (more likely it was the aroma of overcooked corn on the cob at the stand across the way) that did it. The legend of Lundy's is highlighted by the biscuits (unparalleled), the lobsters (always tender), the clams (fresh with the sea taste), the best ice cream (Breyers legendary vanilla), the portions (gigantic).

There had to have been more to it than just the food—spicy, abundant, fresh, well-prepared though it was. It was the moment when food was an extension of social possibility: Chinese food, though a diluted version of Cantonese, was an exotic wonder. Restaurant food, corner food, sodas and frappes, blackout cakes and cream-filled Othellos from Ebinger's, a chain of bakeries whose outlets seemed to be stationed every four or five blocks. From my home I could easily get to the one on Avenue U, the two on Kings Highway, and others on Avenues M and J. Food was evidence of entering into a more generous, sensual world. And it included the unexpected and the seemingly ordinary: a Horn & Hardart's beef pie, like Snow White in her death sleep behind a glass window, released for 35 cents, or seven nickels, placed in an adjoining slot; vegetable cream cheese heaped on a bagel at Dubrow's or Garfield's cafeteria, its price punched on a ticket you pulled from the turnstile when you entered by the man behind the counter; a pizza pie from the Italian neighborhood, which you called in ahead but had to wait for anyway; or a double-decker of corned beef and pastrami on rye with celery tonic from a deli. It was a new world of eats, and from the late twenties through the sixties Lundy's was the great Brooklyn seafood emporium.

Patrons of Lundy's were a rich mix of old Brooklyn and of newcomers who filled the apartment houses along Ocean Avenue and Ocean Parkway and the detached and semidetached houses that lined the numbered streets and alphabetized avenues of Midwood and Sheepshead Bay. So suddenly were these streets created that there was no time to assign names. There were the old families from Prospect Park and the Heights and the mansions and apartment houses of Flatbush—their ancestors filled the plots and elegant mausolea of the spacious groves and hillocks of Greenwood Cemetery—who would travel out to the bay to inhale the ocean air, who could still recall the glory days of the exclusive Manhattan Beach hotels. There were still the old restaurants, but by the late thirties only

Lundy's would be mentioned in restaurant guides as being notable in Sheepshead Bay. And then there were the new Brooklynites from the homes of Midwood and Flatlands and Canarsie—then the suburbs of the city.

Here are the memories of those who ate at Lundy's during these years. Some memories are brief, some lengthy. Often they are contradictory—about the service, the length of time between courses—but all give the feel of conviviality, the sense of high expectation, and the often boisterous atmosphere of dining at Lundy's—the constant sense of celebration, whether it was for an anniversary, birthday, wedding, or an end-of-the-week family treat or ritual. As they tell, it was a place to meet friends, to feel the warmth of a special relationship with a waiter (both waiter and patron ennobled each other in the process). And there are tales of odd behavior: a waiter banging a lobster against the wall, a couple overseeing each other's oral hygiene, or the awkwardness of a first date and a first encounter with a clam, lobster bib, and water bowl after the end of a meal. But all that was part of the grand spectacle of eating at Lundy's.

The oddity is that for all its great size, simple fare, crowds, and noise, Lundy's was not a cold, impersonal restaurant, but was replete with community excitement, curiosity, warmth, and the delirious happiness of a splendid holiday. Lundy's was sometimes infuriating, but it was always fun, and it was the place, as the witnesses below tell us, where memories were made.

GEOFFREY S. HOBART: I remember Lundy Brothers when we moved to Sheepshead Bay in 1945. I was only five years old. The bay was a different place then. The streetcar with polished wood and brass was stationed just opposite Lundy's. Walking into Lundy's was a unique experience. There was that constant clatter of dishes, the din of many voices, the special atmosphere all its own, and the aroma of fresh clams and lobster and hot biscuits. In later years I realized that Lundy's was the only restaurant that could broil a lobster without drying it out. If you entered at Emmons and Ocean Avenues, where the entrance to the new Lundy's is now, the clam bar was just to the right as it is now. And the cocktail lounge was just to the left. On a warm summer day the windows were open and you could order clams on the street side as well as inside. After dinner we sometimes took the ferry to Rockaway and stopped at Kennedy's. As I recall Kennedy's, it was a very old place with grass coming through the floor and a barefoot and shirtless crowd. Kennedy's is still there, but all that has changed. It was sad to lose the ferry through the bay and across the channel. At low tide it sometimes got stuck in the mud. Kids swam from the docks. People would throw coins from the boat, and as the kids retrieved the coins they would proudly show their catch. Through the years I recall Lundy's always had the best clams: never too big, never too small, and always very cold and fresh. My favorite meal was always a dozen littlenecks, lobster bisque with the biscuits, a broiled lobster and baked potato. That was plenty to be satisfied with. There were other restaurants we went to: Pappas, Tappen's, Seidel's, Jenns, Ross-McGuinness, The Barge, Log Cabin, and Ferrara's. All have vanished now. Sometimes after eating we would see a double feature at the Sheepshead Theater or Sheldon Theater, both long gone from Sheepshead Bay Road. But Lundy's was always our favorite to return to.

KEVIN R. McPARTLAND: Lundy's of Sheepshead Bay will always be synonymous with summer and my boyhood in Brooklyn. I can still remember the West Indian waiters in their light green jackets with pink trim. The clatter of silverware and the sound of summer laughter filled the dining room as you entered from Emmons Avenue. The delicious odors permeated the air—the smell of fresh-baked bluefish, soft-shell crabs, and one of my favorites, swordfish steak. It was always on Sunday after a day on the beach at Coney Island that my father would bring me to the restaurant. I was probably eight years old then, but I can remember it like it was yesterday. My father and his friends eating clams and drinking beer from tall thin glasses at the bar. My cousin and I sipping cherry cokes and watching the man behind the bar open clams at a speed that is hard to describe.

DR. LESTER LEVINE: You could say I was virtually brought up in Lundy's; that is, through most of my elementary and high school years, and even through college and professional school years. My parents drove along Ocean Avenue on an average of two to three times each and every week. We all knew a number of the staff members quite well and they knew us. On many occasions the "us" consisted of extended family and close friends.

In the parking lot, Walter or one of his sons greeted us, and whether in freezing weather or in the heat of the summer there was always time to exchange greetings and to review what had taken place in the short intervals preceding each visit.

Once inside, having entered from the Ocean Avenue side of the parking lot, we shifted over one aisle to the right and went directly to either Wattie's or Cooper's table. Mostly it was with the guidance of Pat, the husky, stern-looking, imposing maitre d', who was an ever-helpful and courteous friend to my father.

Wattie and Cooper were just great! My mom and dad and I, being creatures of habit, really didn't need menus, and these waiters always knew what to serve and how we liked it. My father always offered Pat and Wattie or Cooper as well as Walter (outside) a beverage—while he was having one himself—and always brought Wattie and Cooper snow-suits at Christmastime for the youngest members of their families and handbags for their wives. Both Wattie and Cooper attended my father's funeral in 1963. The bonds that developed between these men and our family were very special and will always be held dear to me.

BARBARA WIEDERMAN GOMAR: My memories of Lundy's start as a child of eight. I am sixty-three now, and I remember pulling into a huge parking lot and a fellow taking the car and parking it so close to the next one that I didn't know how he was going to get out. I remember hoping we got there early enough so we didn't have to wait and my parents always trying to get their "special waiter." I could hardly wait for the little warm muffins to come out. I would take a couple home for the next day and would be disappointed when they became hard and tasteless. Next, I remember the steamers. Of course I couldn't even taste them. It was my job to take them out of their shells and wash them in the broth and give them to my dad. I thought that was a fun job. I watched the waiters come out of the kitchen with trays piled high with dinner plates. I always waited for the moment they'd all fall off the tray. Never did I get to witness an accident. I remember my plate being filled by donations of fish and chicken from oversized portions of my family's dinners. As I was a noneater at the time all that was ordered for me was an empty plate. Many, many years later my special memory was as a "young married." Often, a group of ten of us went to dinner there. Many of us ordered the lobster dinner that came with steamers, too many for most of us except my husband, who kept eating and eating, never realizing that we were sneaking our unwanted steamers onto his plate. Finally, he leaned back and sighed, saying, "I can't eat another one. I think they're growing on the plate as I eat them." He realized he was right when he saw us laughing.

HARVEY LUPPESCU: I have three distinct memories of Lundy's. The first is about the old wood Lundy's of the twenties, the next one about the stucco building of the mid-forties, and the last about some strange, yet oddly affectionate behavior my wife and I witnessed. The first takes me back to my childhood about 1926 or '27 when I was three, when my parents would take me there for Sunday dinners. My memory of the physical makeup is vivid. The restaurant was composed of a series of wooden, shack-like structures extending into Sheepshead Bay. A plank bridge led to the first room, and then a series of bridges connected the following rooms. Each of the "shacks" held about twenty-five diners, and to get to the last of the rooms, it was necessary to walk through or around the others on a plank.

Some years ago, when I was in Borneo, I noticed that the huts of a native village were also built on pilings stretching over water. It reminded me of the old Lundy's of the twenties.

My second memory is of a time just after the Second World War. I was living in Rockville Centre then and commuting to the city. It seemed as if every other week there was an interruption of the train service, either because of strikes (very frequent), accidents, track damage. Some friends and I formed a carpool. We'd take the Belt Parkway to Sheepshead Bay and take the subway into the city from there. We always availed ourselves of Lundy's on the way home, meeting at the clam bar for a dozen or so littlenecks as a pre-supper treat.

My third memory of Lundy's is of a couple my wife and I witnessed performing a strange, intimate act at the table. We never attempted the Shore Dinner ourselves—it was gargantuan in quantity—but we watched in awe the couple at the next table polish two of them off. At the conclusion of their meal, the wife leaned over the table with a toothpick and proceeded to remove food particles from her husband's teeth, in accordance with his instructions. Following that, the husband stood up, leaned over, and did the same cleansing job for his wife. It was pretty gauche, to say the least, and the couple were totally oblivious to the rest of the world, yet there was also something deeply loving and caring in the act.

ANDRÉ F. BLOCK: My parents took my brother Charles and me to Lundy's on Sunday afternoons. The crowd was enormous, and we usually parked in one of the additional lots a block or two away. Because of the number of diners, we often had to sit in one of the dining rooms far from the kitchen, and the service there was incredibly slow, but Charles and I were prepared. We brought along a deck of cards and played gin rummy between courses. Often, we managed to complete seven games by the end of a meal.

CLYDE TURNER: Almost all of my family's important milestones, from junior high school to graduate school commencements, were consecrated with a trip down Ocean Avenue to that massive seafood emporium. Although I prided myself and my adolescent appetite in my ability to dispatch a Shore Dinner single-handedly, it was those biscuits that were unequaled anywhere on this planet. I remember being at Lundy's with two aunts who thought they had to smuggle their leftover biscuits out in their umbrellas. They almost panicked when it started to rain as they were leaving. Our waiter rescued them from their dilemma of having either soggy biscuits or ruined hairdos by graciously wrapping their booty in a takeout bag.

JORDAN WEINE: Lamb chops were served with panties. Everything in the interior of the restaurant had turquoise on it, including the waiters' uniforms. They had the best apple pie for takeout on an aluminum plate—a 50-cent deposit was required—that made the best sled. There was an attendant in the bathroom. Mr. Lundy always made sure the salt and pepper shakers were full each night before he retired. If he found fault, the waiter responsible didn't work the next day.

MARTIN GREEN: My son, Steven J. Green, holds the Lundy's record for throwing a spoon from a high chair during a Sunday dinner. At least sixty times! Other memories: Sid Luckman saying hello to me after wearing my cleats at an Erasmus Hall High School football practice earlier in the day; that was in 1941. Food: the biscuits to die for! The raw bar's littlenecks and cherrystones and oysters, fish lobster, "Coney Island" Chowder, and blueberry pie and Breyers ice cream.

LEMUEL COPELAND: In March of 1996, I attended the CIAA basketball tournament in Winston-Salem, North Carolina, a college athletic conference composed of sixteen predominantly black colleges. During a game, I overheard a man behind me telling his friends about working as a waiter one summer in Brooklyn to earn money for his college tuition. He said he was one of the few "American-born colored guys" there and that he had never had enough seafood to eat until he worked in that restaurant. He remembered walking on the bay and watching the fishing boats come in. His wife broke in to say that he always talked of that time and how disappointed she was when on their way to Europe they went out to Sheepshead Bay and found the restaurant shuttered. I knew then that they were talking about Lundy's and I turned around and said, "Buddy, I have some good news for you. Lundy's is back and it has those little biscuits and they are as good as ever." The man screamed with joy and gave me a hug. As soon as the weather broke, he said, they were going to go back.

Front dining room, Lundy Bros. Restaurant, 1935. Photograph by Joseph Rutter. Courtesy of Carol Lundy Bamert.

Outdoor patio dining area on the second level was a summer feature of Lundy's until the late forties, 1935. Photograph by Joseph Rutter. Courtesy of Carol Lundy Bamert.

Roof dining room, Lundy Bros. Restaurant, 1935. Photograph by Joseph Rutter. Courtesy of Carol Lundy Bamert.

Kitchen, Lundy Bros. Restaurant, 1935. Photograph by Joseph Rutter. Courtesy of Carol Lundy Bamert.

Inside bar, Lundy Bros. Restaurant, 1935. Photograph by Joseph Rutter. Courtesy of Carol Lundy Bamert.

Clam bar, Lundy Bros. Restaurant, 1935. Photograph by Joseph Rutter. Courtesy of Carol Lundy Bamert.

Parking lot, Lundy Bros. Restaurant, 1935. Photograph by Joseph Rutter. Courtesy of Carol Lundy Bamert.

RUDOLPH DIPIETRO: Lundy's will live in my wife's and my mind forever, for it was here in 1949 that the seeds were planted to produce a marriage that has lasted since September 27, 1953. I would have to say that it was the long wait for the food that gave us the chance at dinner to make plans for our wedding. We would eat dinner at Lundy's every Saturday night and then go to the Brooklyn Paramount to catch the last show. We remember also McGuinness's restaurant on Emmons Avenue, which served franks with loads of sauerkraut and hot roast beef sandwiches. I personally think that if young couples contemplating marriage would eat at Lundy's, the divorce rate in Brooklyn would be at an all-time low!

LYDIA GREENBLATT: This happened on New Year's Eve in the late sixties: My date and I had ordered the famous Shore Dinner. My lobster was served to me, but it wasn't cracked well enough to get at the meat of the body and claws. We called the waiter over and explained the problem to him. He took my lobster, wrapped it in my dinner napkin, walked to the nearest wall and smashed it against the wall! He returned to our table, unwrapped my dinner, placed it on my plate, and said, "How's that, lady!" That was the essence of Lundy's.

ALLEN MAXFIELD: I was born in 1923 and lived in Flatbush. I can remember eating at Lundy's when it was across the way, built over the water. It was a lot smaller then. For an outing my parents would take the ferry from Sheepshead Bay to Breezy Point and every time we would stop at Lundy's for clams or a dinner. Later I moved to New Jersey, but every Good Friday I would take my young children for a traditional Lundy's lunch, and my two boys ate all of their Shore Dinners from the age of five on.

63

PATRICIA A. HARRIS: I was born and raised on Staten Island and I remember fondly the Sunday excursions on the 69th Street Ferry to enjoy a scrumptious seafood dinner at Lundy's. My wonderful dad absolutely adored the clam bar, which was usually packed six deep with customers anxiously awaiting their freshly shucked clams. He would wolf down five or six dozen littlenecks in a flash and then sit down to a full dinner. He was a zealous diner who reveled in a hearty meal.

PAUL AND LUCILLE PRAGER: The washroom attendant at Lundy's left a dish on the countertop for gratuities. Many toiletry items were put out for the use of the patrons. Our son Robert, who was about four years old, was delighted to use the facilities. Upon returning to the table he stated: "Boy, I liked that place." He unfolded his hand, exposing several coins. "They pay you for going to the toilet."

RITA S. DRUCKER: During the forties, my family and I would go often to Lundy's, but late, after nine in the evening. We had to wait until my father closed his store on Flatbush Avenue, Mac's Men's Shop (it is still there). He would take along his friends and salesmen and favored customers. When we arrived, Chicky would spot us and miraculously a table would appear, a pristine white tablecloth would be spread out, and in a flash, the settings would be in place. Chicky was a short black waiter who seemed to move on roller skates. As we sat down, water was being poured into the glasses and two dozen cherrystone clams would arrive quickly.

All the waiters were efficient, it seemed to me, and the wait for courses was never more than ten minutes. Dad and Chicky loved each other. My dad, a big man, about 5 feet 11 inches, would walk in and hug Chicky, who was about a foot shorter. People turned around and watched. He—my dad—greeted those seated at other tables who frequented his store. Other patrons would come over to say hello to "Mr. and Mrs. Max." His and Mom's drinks would come out first and then Chicky would take everyone else's orders. I believe they were into Southern Comfort then. My brother and I usually got 7UP, the new drink invented in the thirties. Then Chicky would take our food orders. The bread and butter were always plentiful. We had clam chowder, with big hunks of clams, and salad. Then the broiled or boiled lobsters and steak would be served. Dad would always have the catch of the day. I believe the fried onion rings were the most delicious I ever had. They were not oily and very crisp.

Chicky never hovered over us, yet he seemed to know precisely when someone needed more water or something else. For dessert, I got a big scoop of chocolate ice cream and my brother his scoops of half vanilla and half chocolate. Lundy's pies were always fresh. I liked the apple, and Dad had the blueberry when it was in season. Also seasonal was the pumpkin pie, which could not be duplicated.

We never went on Sunday—it was too crowded for us. Yet on June 12, 1955, my wedding reception was held there, in the upstairs section. There were seventy-five of us, and the table was shaped as an E. Our backs were to the view of the bay and Manhattan Beach. Again, it was lobster and steak, and the drinks flowed freely. To everyone's amazement, the headwaiter took our orders without a pad and pencil.

Over the years, we went back, but suddenly Chicky was gone and our presence caused no stir. Then the restaurant closed and we felt an era had come to an end.

GALE ROBINSON GOLDBERG: The first restaurant that I ever ate in was Lundy's. We went there most Sunday nights of my childhood in the forties and fifties—after listening to Tallulah Bankhead's radio program "The Big Show." We always ordered the same thing:

the Shore Dinner. Everybody said it was too much to eat, but we always managed. The clam chowder had to be "Manhattan" (red), followed by steamers, lobster, broiled chicken, french fries, cherry pie à la mode (with butter pecan ice cream). There was never a time when we had less than two baskets of biscuits.

My father, Meyer Robinson, had his winery (Monarch Wine Company, makers of Manischewitz wine) and offices in Bush Terminal. We always used to bring bottles of wine for the parking lot guys, captain, and waiters. We never had to wait for a parking space close to the door or a table downstairs.

The briny smell when we first walked into the restaurant is still in my olfactory memory.

ROBERTA TEMES: I was in junior high school when we moved from the apartment in a Bronx tenement to an apartment in a two-family house on a quiet, tree-lined street in Brooklyn. The first Sunday in our new neighborhood my parents, my sister, and I strolled to Sheepshead Bay and were stunned to see cars—brown cars, blue cars, green cars, convertibles, and limousines too—lined up and down Emmons Avenue apparently engaged in a mysterious waiting ritual. Dad thought the crowd might be waiting to get into "that big restaurant by the sea, Lindy's, is it?"

Mom set him straight: "Lindy's is for cheesecake. Why would all these folks need dessert at this time of day?"

Judy, my sister and the best reader in second grade at P.S. 195, noticed, "Here in Brooklyn they spell Lindy's with a 'u'."

We walked some more, passing Tappen's Seafood Restaurant and the Hamilton House, and noted that neither of them had waiting cars. We returned to "that big restaurant by the sea" to solve the mystery. I was designated the family spokesperson and bravely knocked on the window of a blue and white Bel Air to ask the driver what he was waiting for. He patiently explained that he had driven his family "all the way from Flatbush for our Sunday Shore Dinner at Lundy's. The wife and boys are inside waiting for a table while I'm out here waiting for a parking spot."

Judy and I wangled permission from Mom to peek into Lundy's. Once our eyes adjusted to the dim light we saw rows of crowded tables covered with so many dishes we could barely see the tablecloths, and we saw rows of hungry would-be diners standing impatiently behind rows of occupied chairs.

Walking home, my parents wore their serious faces and talked to each other, not to us. They were proud of their new sunny and spacious four-room apartment. But their notion of upward mobility did not include the strange concept of "eating out." I actually already knew that. While most of my classmates at Shellbank Junior High School bought lunch at Martin's on Nostrand Avenue, I ate across the street at the counter in Ropages's drugstore. Those of us who had nutritious packed-by-Mom sandwiches were permitted to eat there if we ordered the eight-cent egg cream.

So, although we lived within walking distance of Lundy's, my family never joined the Sunday throngs. But I got to experience Lundy's anyway. It was when I turned sixteen. I did not have a Sweet Sixteen party—I was too tall. (Trust me, it's true.) My boyfriend of the moment, Bruce from Brighton, wanted to celebrate the day with me. With money earned at his summer job at Mrs. Stahl's Knishes he invited me to a special birthday lunch at Lundy's. I bought a new dress using my A&S discount—I worked there Thursday nights and Saturdays.

Bruce was careful to walk on the socially correct side, the "gutter" side, as we made our way to Lundy's that afternoon in June. The towel-armed waiter who greeted us and seated us suggested we order clam chowder, served with Lundy's famous biscuits, and steamed lobster. Accustomed to Mom's boiled beef, roast turkey, or meat loaf, lobster was unknown to me. But I hadn't the opportunity to object because the waiter did not wait for an answer to his suggestions. When the food arrived I looked to Bruce for cues. He was a freshman at college; surely, he'd know how to eat this meal. And he did; he went to an out-of-town college.

Now I knew why folks drove far and waited long to eat at Lundy's. The food was superb. The waiter cleared our places, took our dessert orders—this time permitting us to choose for ourselves— and then gave each of us a rather interesting item. It was a clear glass bowl, about the size of a dessert dish, but my blueberry pie à la mode was not in it. Instead it was filled with water and a floating lemon slice. I immediately recalled that when my sophisticated aunt Helen last visited us she mentioned that she enjoyed ending her meals with a cup of hot water with lemon, instead of coffee. What elegance at Lundy's. Without even asking, they knew to bring me the most tasteful of all drinks. And without looking to Bruce for approval, I confidently proceeded to drink all the water from my finger bowl.

ELI MALLON: I was there only once—with my family, around my seventeenth birthday, in June of 1964. I remember it as very noisy and packed with customers. It was not pretentious, compared with what a large Manhattan seafood restaurant might be like. It was classless. I don't remember feeling that it was a place exclusively for either the rich or the poor. I suppose anyone who could afford it was welcome. It was a neighborhood kind of place, but a grand one. That kind of noisy grandeur was so "Brooklyn." It was large, very large. At the time, I thought of it as a Jewish place—part of Brooklyn Jewish life. In retrospect, that could not have been entirely true. We Jews were probably only one of many groups who felt at home in Lundy's. I think that for families who had once been poor but were now "on the way up," it may have seemed fancy. To others who were less comfortable with their working-class backgrounds, it may have seemed crass. I was somewhere in between. Lundy's was not as exotic as the Greenwich Village coffee-houses, but I felt enwrapped by the communal warmth there. I got the feeling from my father that all real New Yorkers had to be familiar with Lundy's. Years later, driving past its empty shell, I could only regret that New York City had lost such a place. Like Ebbets Field, it was part of what gave New York City its soul. It was funky and glorious.

ELLIOT WILLENSKY: Just poking one's head in Lundy's door on any busy evening would lend credence to the assertions that it had 2,800 seats and that on a typical Mother's Day it served 10,000 meals and up to 15,000 on other special occasions. Before the aroma of Shore Dinners could be assimilated, the roar of thousands of conversations all but pushed the new arrival back onto the avenue. Atmospheric, stuccoed, and with lots of deep-red tile floors every-where, the interior guaranteed a ricochet of sound in every direction.

Once inside, one was quickly marched to a table, sometimes out in left field, in an area no more unfamiliar to the guest, you discov-ered, than to the waiters and busboys, who seemed not yet to have found it. The menus were elaborate, detailed, mouthwatering, and, after a period that allowed the menu to be skimmed, were retrieved by the waiter, who would then call you to attention and impatiently demand your order, to be shouted over the din.

Only then did the food begin to arrive, steaming hot, generous in portions, and very, very fresh. It was worth it all. That's why everyone came back for more.

BILL ROSENBERG: Our trips to Lundy's were a much-anticipated Sunday-afternoon ritual. My father had been frequenting Lundy's since it had been located on a pier in Sheepshead Bay, and we knew he was acquainted with one of the Lundy brothers. Over the years he had decided that the rear table in the bar, the one closest to the main dining room, was to be "his" table, and his table continues to have great significance for me. We would arrive at the restaurant at 12:30 P.M., stand outside the black wrought-iron gates, and patiently await their opening at 1:00. To my seven-year-old imagination the interior of the building seemed to be a sultan's palace. Cool, dark corridors led off in all directions to fabulous destinations! Mounds of clams lay on beds of ice behind the clam bar before they were ceremoniously shucked and served up by the barmen. Stairways beckoned, and when explored yielded such exotic sights as the men's room: a cool green place, dimly lit, with rows of gleaming washbasins.

At precisely 1:00 P.M., the gates would swing open, and my father would signal to "his waiter," John, that he had arrived. John would nod, smile, and escort us to that special table. A new odyssey was about to begin! I don't remember John's face, other than the fact that it was, as were those of all the waiters, dark brown. All the Lundy's waiters were black, a not-too-pleasant reminder of the days of Jim Crow, but to me these men were magnificent in their mint green jackets and tan pants with a pink stripe down the side.

All of us would start off with a prelunch drink served by the two gentlemen who ruled the bar, Roger and Paul. Roger, a genial man with a broad florid face, would concoct an array of drinks with great flair as the absolute master of his shakers and implements. He would stir, measure, and shake the drinks and occasionally disappear into a huge walk-in refrigerator behind the bar, returning with all sorts of exotic ingredients. In my family, however, the order was always the same: a Beefeater Gibson for my father, a brandy Alexander for my mother, and for me one of Roger's "specials": a ginger ale with a maraschino cherry. Apparently, Roger made such an impression on me with the quality of his Shirley Temple that when I turned eighteen, I went to him for my first "real" drink.

After the drinks, the biscuits arrived, hot and soft so that the butter would melt and run dripping down the sides. Along with the biscuits came a type of hardtack cracker, but I always charged after the biscuits despite my mother's warning that I might spoil my appetite. We all ate far too many of them and would have to signal John for more. Then the menus came. My father would always start with a wonderful lump crabmeat cocktail, while my mother and I settled for shrimp cocktails. For their main course, my parents chose broiled lobsters. They were able to dismember them with real skill, but that deftness was beyond me and I timidly chose the lamb chops.

My father had a second Gibson, but my mother giggled that her drink had gone straight to her head. Then the food arrived—a feast of huge portions. Our entrées were complemented by gigantic side orders of Lyonnaise potatoes and green peas. We attacked the mounds of food and usually managed to reduce them from mountains to small hillocks, at which point we would lean back in our chairs. Of course we weren't finished—not without slabs of blueberry pie, coffee for the folks, and milk for me. At just about this time, a tall gaunt man in a blue sportcoat would stop at our table and chat with my father. When he left, I always asked who he was. My dad would say: "That's Mr. Lundy," and I'd be so proud that my father knew the man who owned this magnificent restaurant. Often, friends of my parents would stop by, and it seemed as though all of Brooklyn passed through the doors of Lundy's at one time or another.

My father passed away twenty years ago. How I wish he could

71

have been with me to witness the reopening of the restaurant. I went to the restaurant in early February with my fiancée (now my beloved wife), Chris. Much had changed, yet there was also so much that was recognizable. When we arrived, the restaurant was jammed, not a table to be had. Finally the hostess lead us through the crowd, and I thought again of my father and all those Sunday afternoons. When we reached our destination, I felt goose bumps—we were standing directly in front of what my father called his table! When I told this to Chris she too felt the eerie sensation of another presence. Coincidence? Maybe, but we toasted the memory of my father, and we sensed the beginning of a new chapter in the saga of Lundy's and the Rosenberg family.

ROZ FELDMAN: Our neighborhood, East New York, literally sang forth with the warm, friendly camaraderie that existed among our people. This was also reflected in one of our favorite weekend restaurants, Lundy's. It was just about the largest restaurant we had ever seen. Not only was the main floor a full block in distance but there was also another level one flight up that ran the entire block, and it was busy! We would walk through the restaurant to determine which table would be leaving soon, and we would wait near that table for the people to leave; and then it was ours. The hot biscuits on the table were a family favorite—not too salty or buttery—and their appearance meant we would be served. I always marveled at the distance some of the waiters had to carry the food to the table being served. The food was always fresh and delicious, and Lundy's was a fun place for us. We didn't need a special occasion to eat there. We just dropped in and enjoyed ourselves. It was a great blow to us when Lundy's closed, because it signaled the end of a cherished era. We love having it back.

BRUCE DANBROT: Was there ever a bigger, more wonderful restaurant than Lundy's? No, there was not!

When people talk about Lundy's, they all remember the splendid architecture, the wonderful Shore Dinners, the reasonable prices, the biscuits, the pie à la mode, the metal trays that you would leave a five-cent deposit on when your mom would ask you to bring home a blueberry pie, the very active waiters scurrying around to accommodate the multitude of customers, the circling of tables when you sensed a party of five was about to leave. All those memories were shared by everyone that ever ate there, but I have some very special memories, most good, one bad. The good ones include my mother and father making Lundy's part of my life when I was about five years old; then twenty years later introducing Lundy's to the woman who would become my wife; then introducing our daughter, Lisa, to Lundy's when she was about five years old. Then comes the bad memory: Lundy's closing down. That big, beautiful restaurant remained standing, deteriorating with time like an ancient relic, with all sorts of rumors that someday it would return. Lundy's became the Brooklyn Dodgers of restaurants, but unlike Ebbets Field and the Dodgers, it did come back. Now I can look forward to introducing my grandchild to Lundy's.

TAMARA ENGEL: The biscuit pyramids at Lundy's were as much an architectural symbol of our borough as the Brooklyn Bridge. The butter pats came on white squares of paper, gently folded up on all four sides, and the biscuits were warm enough for the butter to melt on contact. The thick, golden-brown Manhattan clam chowder—with plenty of clams, potatoes that were not too soft, and more than a hint of thyme—was delicious. This was the way to begin every dinner, especially the Shore Dinner.

73

Now Lundy's was not a perfect place. We had our complaints. It was the best fish restaurant, but we didn't like the catch-as-catch-can way of lassoing a table. There was no hostess, maitre d', or numbering system for seating. If we saw a free table, it was a running dash to claim it. If no table was available, more often than not we found one where the people were eating dessert and hovered over them to claim it next.

My father had a system of his own. We'd send him in first to scan the room for a familiar face. Nine out of ten times he'd spot one, and that secured the table. I have vivid memories of him pulling up a chair to a table and schmoozing with an old crony from Williamsburg, while we waited on the sidelines. As teenagers, my sister, brother, and I hated being introduced to strangers, but it was a price we were willing to pay for a fried shrimp dinner.

Service at Lundy's was hit or miss, and we often needed seconds of biscuits and the oysterette crackers already on the table before our clam chowder arrived.

When I was sixteen, my steady boyfriend had something to give me for my birthday—a lobster. We walked in through one of Lundy's many side entrances and found ourselves in the cavernous salmon-and-turquoise-colored dining room. The waiter helped me tie my little bib. I followed my boyfriend's lead and began with the claws. Ecstasy! Over the years I think we two held the record for taking the longest time to eat lobsters. Then came the finger bowl—elegant and needed. (From *The Brooklyn Cookbook* by Lyn Stallworth and Roderick Kennedy, Jr. Copyright © 1991 by Lyn Stallworth and Roderick Kennedy, Jr. Reprinted by permission of Alfred A. Knopf.)

WENDY WASSERSTEIN: In the early days of my family, we sometimes officially celebrated Mother's Day. We ventured en masse in the mid-fifties to Lundy's restaurant in Sheepshead Bay, Brooklyn, for seafood. According to my mother, it was a beautiful occasion. My grandmother wore a corsage, and the children looked beautiful and were beautifully behaved. I on the other hand recall a vast, dark medieval hall where waiters shoved by with plates piled high with steamers and lobster tails, and my brother and I tossed hot biscuits. (Copyright © 1989 by the New York Times Co. Reprinted by permission.)

ROBERT CORNFIELD: Lundy's was part of my life from my earliest years—it was as familiar a presence as the Nostrand trolley, the Avenue R temple, or the children's section of the Kingsway movie theater. It was a long walk or a short bike ride from home, though when the family went my father drove.

On Sundays we ate either at the "Chinks"—that derogatory term was intended more as shorthand description than contemptuous superiority—more appropriately known as Honam's Chinese Restaurant near Kings Highway and Coney Island Avenue, or at Lundy's. At Honam's, my brothers and I would swap parts of our combination dinners: for instance, my eldest brother, Larry, would trade his fried rice for my spare ribs, or I would get an extra egg foo yung for the shrimp off my shrimp chow mein. Eddy, the difficult middle child, let me have his wonton soup for my egg roll. By the time my father furiously slammed a halt to this bartering we all felt cheated of something. No shenanigans were allowed at Lundy's.

For us Lundy's was invariably a late Sunday afternoon business, with my mother taking up most of the getting-ready-to-go-out preparation time. By the time she cautiously high-heeled her way down the brick front stairs, we had been piled in the 1939 Plymouth with the motor running for some time. Dottie Citron called from her porch across the street to ask why we were all so dolled up, and Mother told her with a touch of pride that we were going to Lundy's. Well, Dottie and Sid had been there earlier, with their kids Carol and Larry, and the place was jammed. We'd never get in. Mother told her we weren't in any hurry, and if we couldn't get in we'd go to Pappas, which my father preferred anyway (this wasn't true).

Depending on who we had been playing with earlier, or who had come over for a visit ("Look, Aunt Faye and Uncle Abe are here!" "So, how come you didn't call?" "We were just driving around. We took a chance." "You want to come with us to Lundy's?" "Poo. I can't take that noise and the crowd. I wouldn't wait on line for any-thing. You go. Don't worry about us. Sunday, I'd rather eat at home."), there might be a small crowd with us: Larry's girlfriend Gloria from Bedford Avenue or my friends from 27th Street, André and Joel, with whom I walked home or to school for over six years, figuring how to blow up the school, steal a copy of an exam, or kill a teacher.

The car discussion was about how maybe we should try parking on the street, not too far away from the restaurant. My father would drop us off, and we would secure the table. The terror here was that Daddy would be circling the streets like the Flying Dutchman for-ever, unable to find a spot, and the waiter would come for our order and Dad still would not have appeared. Also, wouldn't they know that we had disobeyed the unspoken rules and parked elsewhere? Dad joined the parking lot line and eventually abandoned the Plymouth to the attendant.

The area of the restaurant that had been decided upon was the far western part of the Emmons Avenue side. Eating at Lundy's was a battleground: getting the car parked, getting a table, getting the waiter's attention, having the food served, staying in place while the next shift of hungry vultures hovered. The reward was the bounty of food: those biscuits—the most fondly recalled item.

I remember a headwaiter or traffic manager who, to maintain some semblance of order, would indicate what section to try for a free table, but there we would search by ourselves for the next likely free table and hover, staking it out and fending off intruders. There was something of the confusion of a battle as the busboys tried to clear off and set up while we grabbed the chairs. The menus were dealt down the table as we tried to decipher whether the waiter was sympathetic or belligerent. Nothing could be more businesslike or unsentimental than the way he marked down our choices on his order card.

We all wanted the chowder and steamers and french fries, and for the kids it was fried clams and for my mother lobster au gratin and my father a lobster. Sharing was obligatory. Everyone had to taste everyone else's and we ate fast. The room's clatter and roar didn't encourage conversation, and all that was discussed was who wanted what. Dessert was a mess of blueberry pies with vanilla ice cream, and we groaned our ways out the door, maybe to work it off with a walk around the bay or across the wooden bridge that led to Manhattan Beach. Usually, Larry didn't hang around and went off somewhere, and Eddy set off on foot to a Bedford Avenue playground. For my parents and me the day would be topped off with a movie (one I had already seen Saturday afternoon, but I was insatiable) at the Avenue U or Nostrand or Avalon or Kingsway or Mayfair. At the end of one Lundy's meal, Larry and Gloria took me off with them to see *Gone With the Wind* at Brooklyn's most extravagant movie palace, the Loews Kings on Flatbush. Could the splendor of eating in the world's largest restaurant, then moving on to see the most luxuriant and endless technicolor movie of all time, in a colossal, ornate, echoing theater be equaled at any time in history? In Brooklyn, we lived magnificently.

77

Roland Hill, Once a Lundy Waiter

All memories of Lundy's include the waiters—they are remembered as brusque, efficient, strong, polite, curt, imposing, terrifying, helpful, intimidating, vanishing, family friends, unsentimental. They had all these qualities and they are crucial to the life and experience of Lundy's. For many patrons, the waiters embodied their first experience of service—and diners wanted to be both worthy of service, yet be in control, not be intimidated, nor did they want to be bullying or undemocratic.

An all-black staff was a familiar feature of top-notch restaurants—the vestiges of the servant tradition—and the blacks took it as a measure of both pride and ability. The Pullman porters became a union rallying point in the twenties. In New York, black waiters were a tradition, especially in seafood establishments: notable in Manhattan was the Gloucester House and the Coach House, and in Brooklyn, Gage & Tollner's. As late as 1964 a promotion booklet for Gage's read: "Today, as in the past, the service at Gage & Tollner's is as distinctive as the food served and is reminiscent of plantation days in the old South. It is provided by affable Negro gentlemen who take pride in remembering not only customers' names, but often their particular preference in dishes as well." At Gage's the waiters wore sleeve insignia indicating their years of service: a gold bar was one year; a gold star, five years; a gold eagle, twenty-five years.

Roland Hill worked as a waiter at Lundy's from the mid-thirties until he was drafted in 1943. He served in an all-black unit of the Aviation Engineers, building roads through the Himalayas and airstrips in Burma. In the late forties he joined Gage & Tollner's, the famed downtown Brooklyn restaurant, and he left there in 1970. He was vice president of Local 2 of the Hotel and Dining Room Workers

Union. Active in Sheepshead Bay community affairs, he lives in a house his father-in-law built in the area.

ROLAND HILL: In 1936, I came up from South Carolina. I was born and reared on what was known as the Clinton Plantation, near Lancaster. At one time, my father oversaw the local cotton mill and corn mill and sawmill on behalf of the bank, who had taken over their management from the owner, Jim Crawford. I would play with the owner's son, Leroy, a year younger than me, jumping into the baling pits, until one day Crawford told my father that it's time that Roland starts calling Leroy "Mister." I was nineteen and my father wanted me to get away from the strict segregation of the South and get into politics and then come back home. I went to live with an aunt and my cousins on 16th Street in Sheepshead Bay until I could establish myself. There was a tradition of blacks coming to this area that went back to the years of the racetracks and great restaurants and hotels. For instance, all the waiters at Tappen's came from Hillsboro, North Carolina. When I got there, there was a substantial well-to-do black community. It was known as the COPSIC area: Committee of the Preservation of a Self-Integrated Community. My neighbor's house was built by a famous horse trainer, Mr. Newton, and his son was a famous jockey. In the thirties, the rest of Sheepshead Bay was mostly Irish and Italian, but after the war it became mostly Jewish. Now the Asians have moved in. Avenue U is like a little Chinatown.

Cousins worked at Lundy's and they got me a job—I arrived in Brooklyn at one o'clock and was at work at five. Friday, Saturday, Sunday, we worked a minimum of twelve hours: we'd get there at eleven and finish up either at midnight or one. Weekdays, the night shift would show up at four and work till midnight. Lundy gave us red jackets to wear, and since there was no air-conditioning, we'd have to change them several times during the day. No break. We had one day a week off. Most of us lived in Harlem, so we had an hour-and-a-half train trip each way. You took the A train to Franklin Avenue, then the Franklin shuttle to Prospect Park, and then the BMT to Sheepshead Bay. Later, I got a room there too. For most of the weekend waiters this was a second job—to put the kids through school, to put yourself through school. Decoration Day through Labor Day was the high season, the additional waiters were college kids from the South working for tuition.

Lundy was a fanatic about the quality of the food. It had to be the best, and the service had to be the best. In the kitchen, there were three sections: the lobster section, the soup section, and the fish section. On weekends there were two men whose only job was to kill the lobsters and put them on racks. The lobsters were all two-pounders. He didn't deal in small ones. The steaks and the chops were the best you could get, and you're turning out at least five hundred steaks a day.

Lundy required that you had a minimum of fourteen seats. We had trays we called Big Berthas, giant-sized ones, because let's say you had a party of six, and they were all having the Shore Dinner. You'd be carrying from almost a block away six orders of steamers covered with heavy bowls and the butter and broth. During the summer 60 percent of the customers would order watermelon for dessert, and they'd each get one-fourth of a melon. And with six people you'd have close to two watermelons on a tray.

Once the customers sat down they'd immediately start calling for the rolls. Some of them called them hot chestnuts. "Bring some hot chestnuts!" The bake shop was going continually.

For a waiter to get a good station, nearer the kitchen, you had to tip the headwaiter. We had what was known as the board. Well, Chick Stevens was the headwaiter there for years and years. He would take this board that had slots for little slips with the waiters' names and walk around with it when the waiters came to work at four, giving them their place assignments. You got there early so you could see Chick and find out where you're going to work. I'd go over to check and ask, "Whatcha have, Cap?" And he says, "Ohhhhh, I have something for you, over on Ocean Avenue." "Aw, come on, Cap." "OK, OK, OK, what *you* got?" So you slip him $5. And he'd take the slip and put you nearer to the kitchen. You'd have to go through this every day. But there were some waiters downstairs that had permanent stations.

At that time, in the mid-thirties, you were happy you had a job. You had a better-than-average income for most blacks, but you lived under the fear of ever doing something wrong. Lundy would just look at you and say, "You're fired." Not that he was cruel, it was that his requirements for work were so strict. He was an absolute dictator. You lived in fear. You never had the feeling that tomorrow I'll still have this job. He'd come in on Thursday—the rest of the week he was at his country place, and somebody would tell him that one of us had done something. He fired me once because he was strict about you not eating any of his food, other than what he prepared for you. A cook had slipped me an egg sandwich, and, standing there on the walkway, he saw me and said, "Come up here! Where'd you get that egg?" "I got it downstairs." "Okay, you won't eat here anymore. You're fired." Five weeks later he sent for me. I guess I finished my punishment. You have to realize that back then blacks working at Lundy's—90 percent of them couldn't get a job anyplace. Here we were, making a darn good income but working like slaves. All his life Lundy fought off any effort by the waiters to unionize. Any time the waiters threatened to strike, he would threaten to shut down the restaurant forever. Finally, for one year in the sixties the union got in, but then the next year under pressure from Lundy the waiters decided they didn't want to stay in the union, and that was the end of that.

5

The Later Years

From the thirties through the early sixties, Lundy's was jammed on weekends, full during the week; it could be said that much of Brooklyn grew up eating clams and lobsters there. It was a successful and famous institution that whatever its behind-the-scenes troubles always kept up appearances and didn't fail its customers. There was mutual loyalty, and the restaurant continued to stand for the best of Brooklyn living. But Brooklyn was being undermined by social forces—the move by a substantial segment of the middle class to the suburbs, and the consequent loss of industry—the impact of which wouldn't be fully realized until the early seventies.

During the thirties and forties Irving Lundy managed to buy up all the property along Emmons Avenue, and there were no complaints from his tenants—so many of whom were other restaurateurs. The neighborhood's next change after the expansion of Emmons Avenue and the rebuilding of the docks in the early thirties came in 1940 with the completion of the Belt Parkway, called the Circumferential

Allen Lundy. Courtesy of Carol Lundy Bamert.

Highway during its construction, which circled Brooklyn and gave the borough quick access to southern Long Island.

Robert Moses wanted access roads on both sides of the parkway, but in granting the section of land that Lundy controlled for the parkway Lundy negotiated for the south access road space to be used for his parking lot. He cut a deal, which the city went along with to avoid a prolonged court case, and the access road had a rude interruption on the Lundy block. Not until the restaurant was sold in the early 1980s was this spur of the access road taken over by the city. In 1941, the same Justice Charles Lockwood who had determined the amounts due to those who had their property taken for the widening of Emmons Avenue awarded $2,395,874 to the owners of the land and property that had been taken for the Sheepshead Bay portion of the Belt Parkway. The last claim was settled at 5:30 P.M. on May 29, and twelve hours later, at 5:30 A.M. on May 30, Robert Moses opened the Belt Parkway.

The highway's path cut a swath through the Sheepshead Bay neighborhood and the continuity of its north-south streets was interrupted. Underpasses were established at ten-block intervals, at Ocean Parkway, and Ocean Avenue, but the community suffered both a physical and psychological divide. Nearly all of Bath Beach was virtually destroyed and Bay Ridge and Fort Hamilton lost easy access to the shore. To make up for this, the Coney Island Beach was expanded into Brighton, adding eighteen acres of former private property, and the boardwalk was also extended, with a final push to the border of Manhattan Beach coming at the end of the forties. To the west, the Moses plan was to eliminate the honky-tonk character of Coney Island by killing off by neglect the amusement areas, and to make Coney a domesticated version of his great beaches at Jones Beach and Riis Park.

Moses's master concept was influenced by a regional plan drafted by the Russell Sage Foundation in the twenties for a Greater New York area linked by superhighways. Its implementation was hastened by the public works projects of the Depression, interrupted by the Second World War, then reached its fulfillment in the postwar years. For the boroughs, the worst effect of the full implementation of the master plan was the encouragement of industry to leave the city for the spaces of the suburbs.

The drive that had fueled the movement out of the tenements of Manhattan to the boroughs was passed along to the next generation, who sought to find more spacious and comfortable living in subur-

A portrait of Frederick William Irving Lundy. Photograph by James Franco. Courtesy of Allen Lundy.

ban communities. Beginning in the mid-fifties and continuing into
the seventies there was a pileup of disasters for Brooklyn: the flight
of the Dodgers, the collapse of the downtown area, the loss of local
industry, the destabilization of shoreline communities, the deliberate
destruction of many communities by neglect and ill-conceived housing developments. The myth of the dirty, dangerous, harried, and
stunting life of the city grew. While the dream of more spacious living was fulfilled, there remained for those who had left Brooklyn a
hankering for a Nathan's hot dog, the Sunday crowds at Lundy's,
back-alley stickball or stoopball, post-Broadway runs at the Flatbush
and Brighton Theaters, the trolley ride to Loehmann's or the excited
push through the Ebbets Field entrances.

By the mid-sixties, it seemed as if those who had left the city and
its boroughs had taken industry with them. Many Brooklynites took
to the roads and settled in the wilds of Jersey and Long Island, and
the newcomers to the borough found that the jobs had fled with
them. The flourishing opportunities of city life were gone—and so
was its value. It was, as Marshall Berman calls it, "a reconstruction
of the whole fabric of America." Berman says that the emphasis on
the automobile as the vehicle for happy suburban living "conceived of
cities principally as obstructions to the flow of traffic, and as junk-
yards of substandard housing and decaying neighborhoods from
which Americans should be given every chance to escape."

This desertion left behind too much that was of immense benefit
to a sense of community, continuity, and real variety in social living.
For, from its Brownsville tenements to its Ocean Parkway apartment
houses to its Flatbush and Bay Ridge mansions to its new Midwood
housing, Brooklyn for more than a quarter of the twentieth century
had been glamorous, fabulous in its variety and vigor. Lundy's restaurant had been a prominent statement of that kind of people's glamour.

Overview of Sheepshead Bay, 1948. Courtesy of Brian Merlis.

In 1948 Lundy had bought Tappen's restaurant—which had been in the hands of one family for 103 years. Tappen's was founded in 1845, on a property on Emmons between East 26th and 27th Streets, before it moved to the former site of the old Villepigue's on Voorhies and Ocean Avenues. Two years later, the building was destroyed in a fire. The Hamilton House, a branch of the famous Bay Ridge restaurant, now Tio's, had taken over Billy Sheirr's roast beef restaurant on Ocean Avenue and Shore Road, and that was to close also. The best places were slowly going.

With Irving Lundy brooking no interference, the management and direction of the restaurant remained in strong family hands. Allen Lundy, who had managed the restaurant from its inception, brought his son in as an apprentice when Allen Jr. was thirteen. Walter Lundy, a cousin, ran the parking lot, and Irving tyrannized them all with lightning appearances. After Allen's death in 1974, his brother-in-law George Higgins took over the management, but with less of Allen's obsessive concern for detail—Carol Bamert and Allen Jr. recall seeing their father at home only once a week, though vacations were spent at the upstate Lundy spread in Wawarsing.

Lundy remained determined that he would run his restaurant his way. But labor demands became more vocal and insistent. Things came to a dramatic pass when in the first week of July 1957 seventy-five waiters walked off their jobs and were followed the next day by two hundred others. They wanted a union. The restaurant stayed open the first weekend with a skeleton staff, but Irving decided that he had had it and shut down the restaurant. It was Allen Lundy who made the announcement, saying that Irving felt the restaurant's standards could not be maintained under these circumstances and the better course would be to close. When asked when it would reopen, Allen answered, "Never!" A week later the waiters began to reappear, and the restaurant reopened without a fuss.

In 1958 Henry Linker, Lundy's only intimate friend from the twenties, suffered a fatal heart attack while playing golf. The loss was a devastating one for Irving, and his characteristic reserve became a defense against any kind of direct communication. He seemed to have made a distinction between family and friend; because his family depended upon him he felt he could not fully confide in them. Linker was not family and had weathered the scrutiny and Lundy's distrust. He had proven over the years to be a loyal confidant. It was a strange kind of isolation; according to Irving's nephew Allen Lundy Jr., Irving's most vulnerable aspect was where he placed his trust and where he didn't. At the end of his life, he gave his trust to those who betrayed it. Irving Lundy began to be a ghostly presence in his own domain, emerging only at dawn, avoiding his family, sending messages through intermediaries.

The seventies were a turbulent time for the restaurant and the Lundy family. The restaurant seemed a constant target for theft and threats. In September 1972, George Higgins, a Lundy nephew, was shot in the abdomen and his son Bruce pistol-whipped in a 1 A.M. robbery attempt. George was thereafter in a state of constant anxiety, fearful of another incident. In November 1974, the restaurant was burglarized again, and this time $30,000 was taken. Less than a month later, another attempted robbery took a bizarre turn. Four masked men broke into the restaurant at 2:25 A.M. and handcuffed two of the night porters. Hearing the commotion, George ordered his uncle to shut himself in his room and then barricaded himself behind a door and started shooting. Passing police heard the noise and ran to the restaurant, causing the thieves to flee, but Higgins refused to believe that those shouting to him that all was safe were actually the police and kept firing. This went on for three hours and three officers were slightly wounded. Finally, Frank Wright, a retired policeman whom Higgins had known, was located and convinced Higgins, who later admitted he had had a couple of drinks, to come out. Lundy's fourteen Irish setters kept up a racket during the night's shootings, but Lundy himself claimed to have slept through it all and refused to accompany Higgins to the police station.

This was not the end of horrendous events: in July of the following year, three men managed to find the entrance to Lundy's bedroom, where after tying him up they ransacked the room, taking two diamond horseshoe pins and a diamond-studded badge. Lundy was the only one who refused to believe someone on the inside might be helping and advising these perpetrators. This state of denial on

Lundy's part was to provide impetus for an escalating series of violent attacks and deceptions.

On September 19, 1975, Bob Thiele, Athenaise Lundy's son, received a pleading and frightened telephone call from his aunt Elaine, the youngest Lundy sister, who lived next door to his mother in Forest Hills. He drove out with his wife, the singer Teresa Brewer, found that his mother was safe, and then went next door. In the living room he discovered the body of his uncle George Higgins Sr., who shared a house with Elaine. Higgins had died of suffocation after being bound and gagged, and the house had been ransacked.

Tappen's, Ocean and Voorhies Avenues, 1948. The former Villepigue's (compare with page 15), the inn taken over by Tappen's. Last owned by Irving Lundy, it was destroyed by fire in 1950. Photograph by Hesse Brothers. Collection of The Brooklyn Historical Association.

Thiele immediately called the police, who in searching the rest of the house found Elaine in a rear room shot in the head. What had they been searching for? Rumors were that Irving hid large amounts of cash in the walls of his restaurant, in the basements of his Long Island estates, and by implication maybe in the houses of his sisters. Or was this retribution for Lundy's suspected refusal to pay kickbacks? Or a warning to the intended target?

Weeks before, when Elaine had come to the restaurant, Irving had ordered her to leave and to never set foot inside again—not out of any hostility but because he feared for her life. To his mind, Elaine had been killed for her safe deposit key. He said to one family member that his baby sister had been murdered because of the family money.

It seemed obvious that there must be a connection between the robberies and these brutal murders, and though there were suspicions everywhere, once again Irving Lundy refused to offer any theory or to cooperate in any further investigation. It had been Irving's way to fight off reality by utter denial and avoidance. The restaurant troubles piled up: in 1976 forty illegal aliens who were working at Lundy's were arrested by U.S. Immigration and Naturalization Service agents.

After the killings of his sister and her husband, Lundy feared not only for his safety but for Marion Anderson's, a trusted employee. He would call her at home after she left the restaurant to be sure she had arrived safely. The next morning there would be another call to be reassured that she had had a safe night. But he would never engage in conversation with her husband or children. When she ate at the restaurant, a special table was prepared for her and her guests, and his thoughtfulness was so overwhelming that her husband was embarrassed to eat there. She was not the only beneficiary of his generosity, for she became his emissary to local hospitals when he heard of any old bay resident who was ill. He covered their hospital costs; when his tenants in the houses and restaurants along Emmons Avenue were low in funds, he allowed them to skip the rent. Helen Randazzo has often told how he provided the funds for her family restaurant.

In his later years, he confided to her that the restaurant was a losing proposition—the patrons were still there, but costs rose when the prices did not. He would not think of closing—where else would his loyal staff find other employment? He was their support, and he felt that his commitment to the community would not allow him to shut down, and then again, what would happen to the bay without Lundy's? To give it all up was unthinkable. As it was, the neighborhood of set-back, verandaed Victorian homes, of small cottages, of empty fields was disappearing, first cut through by the Belt Parkway, then by the appearance east of Nostrand Avenue of high-rise developments. It was no longer a neighborhood with hints of a faded grandeur; even the suggestions became more elusive.

What Lundy hoped was to keep Sheepshead Bay's feel of a small fishing village with tackle and bait shops, restaurants and clam bars, fishing boats, promenades. He had been trying to hold the area together since the twenties, and he felt he could do this by buying up all the local property. His extravaganza of a seafood restaurant was the linchpin, but what surrounded it had to be in appropriate relationship.

In the early seventies, Lundy wanted to create a theater, playground, and store complex on Emmons to halt the street's deterioration. Lundy asked Herb Shalat, who had taken over the architectural firm that had originally designed the restaurant and oversaw all of its changes, to draw up a plan, but the city fought him with zon-

*Front entrance, Lundy Bros. Restaurant, 1950. Photograph by Hess Brothers.
Collection of The Brooklyn Historical Association.*

ing regulations, and the project came to nothing. In late 1996, the
same plot was developed for a Sheepshead Bay Loehmann's—with
the city granting the developers all that had been denied Lundy and
Shalat.

Lundy felt safe only in his barren, undecorated apartment, or in
the secure back corridors of the restaurant, or in the kitchen. In the
kitchen he would have Kirk, the salad chef, cut up the food for his
fourteen Irish setters from the best of the restaurant's provender. On
alternate days, his chauffeur and bodyguard, Ciro Autorino, would
take a different group of dogs to be exercised on his Long Island

estates. The rest of the time they had their run in the back area of the restaurant. His will offered $10,000 for each dog who was adopted, but the lot of them were wildly out of control—inbred, high-strung, untamable—and all found resting places in a pet cemetery in Queens.

On the evening of September 6, 1977, Ciro Autorino told Walter Lundy that he had found Irving slumped over his desk, his face sunk into a pillow, dead. Lundy was eighty-two. The medical examiner stated that he had died of a heart attack. After his death, his closets were found to be full of brown suits and slacks—all brown, all carefully wrapped in tissue paper, most unworn from the day of purchase. But that was to be the least of the surprises. The inheritors were Lundy's niece and nephews Carol Bamert, Allen Lundy, Bob Thiele, and George Higgins. At the Wawarsing farm, the caretaker Frank Ek was approached by a man who claimed to be the new owner. It had been sold to him by Irving Lundy himself, who the man described as forty and short. Fred and Carol Bamert, and Allen and his wife, Valerie, took immediate action. The disguise turned out to be the tip of the iceberg. Lundy, it turned out, had been embezzled of $11 million during the eight months prior to his death. The New York *Daily News* noted that this was the largest embezzlement, involving the assets of a single individual, in the United States. District Attorney Eugene Gold announced in February 1979 that there had been a $500,000 cash theft from a vault at Lundy's mansion in Brookville. At Lundy's instruction, money and valuables had been carted there in lobster crates. The embezzlers' transfers of money, stock, and property had involved international trafficking between Uruguay, Switzerland, Panama, and New York. Indeed, it was the property deeds that were at the center of the deceptions. Six men were indicted for conspiracy to defraud, but only four were put on trial: Ciro Autorino, Joseph Ramaglia, Eric Coursen, and Mark Stellato. Mario Caliari, an Italian citizen, appeared as a witness, and Stellato plea-bargained. The most serious conspirator was Lundy's chauffeur and confidant, Ciro Autorino, who engineered that thousands of acres of Lundy property be placed in a trust fund with a Lundy impostor signing Lundy's name. It was Ramaglia who had passed himself off as Lundy in Upstate New York. Total fines for the four totaled $600,000, and they all received jail sentences.

For two years, the new owners struggled to reinvigorate the old restaurant. Bob Thiele even wrote a song with George David Weiss for his wife to record in order to promote Sheepshead Bay:

> Sleepy seagulls stirrin'
> Fishin' boats a bobbin'
> Sunrise floatin' closer
> A brand-new day
> and I am home again in Sheepshead Bay . . .

It was not a hit.

The restaurant was closed in 1979 by order of the executor and was then sold along with fourteen acres of nearby property in 1981 for a reputed $11 million to the Litus Group. For the next fourteen years plans for a new restaurant, a nightclub, a high-rise hotel, to make the building the center of a South Street Seaport complex of shops and restaurants, came and went, and during these years the furnishings lay intact but decaying within the shuttered building.

Old patrons would drive out, hoping that it had reopened, but all they found was a shuttered shell. It was awful. Where had those great years gone? What had happened?

6

Lundy's Reborn

Throughout the eighties, the empty Lundy's building stood as one of the few remaining indications of better times. Local efforts to seek landmark status for the building grew, and with only slight opposition Lundy's restaurant was recognized by New York's Landmarks Preservation Commission as a significant monument worthy of preservation. In 1991, the building was then granted this status. Here is the official designation description made by the commission:

On the basis of a careful consideration of the history, the architecture and other features of this building, the Landmarks Preservation Commission finds that the F.W.I.L. Lundy Brothers Restaurant Building has a special character, special historical and aesthetic interest and value as a part of the development, heritage and cultural characteristics of New York City.

The Commission further finds that, among its important qualities, the F.W.I.L. Lundy Brothers Restaurant Building is

Lundy Bros. Restaurant, 1960. Compare with page 42. The outdoor second-level dining area has been enclosed. Another addition was a single-story extension of the clam bar area on Ocean Avenue, known as the Teresa Brewer Room. It was demolished before the recent renovation. Collection of The Brooklyn Historical Society.

the last of the great seafood palaces which once flourished in Sheepshead Bay, a shorefront community known for its fishing fleet and famous eating places; that the building was constructed in 1934 for restaurateur Frederick William Irving Lundy in conjunction with the government-sponsored redevelopment of the Sheepshead Bay waterfront in the mid-1930s; that it was thought to be one of the largest restaurant buildings in Brooklyn; that Lundy's became a major Brooklyn institution which served as many as a million meals a year and is remembered fondly by tens of thousands of New Yorkers; that the Lundy Brothers Restaurant Building was designed by the prominent firm of Bloch & Hesse which specialized in restaurant design; that it is a fine example of Spanish Colonial Revival design and exhibits such characteristic features of the style as sand-colored stuccoed walls, low sloping red Mission tile roofs, arched entrances, arcuate corbel tables, decorative ironwork, and leaded-glass windows; that Lundy's was a rare manifestation of the style in a restaurant building and today appears to be the sole survivor of the style among pre–World War II restaurant buildings in New York City.

Accordingly, pursuant to the provisions of Chapter 74, Section 3020 (formerly Section 534 of Chapter 21), of the Charter of the City of New York and Chapter 3 of Title 25 of the Administrative Code of the City of New York, the Landmarks Preservation Commission designates as a Landmark the F.W.I.L. Lundy Brothers Restaurant Building, 1901–1929 Emmons Avenue, Borough of Brooklyn, and designates Borough of Brooklyn Tax Map Block 8775, Lot 41, as its Landmark Site.

Lundy's became an officially celebrated monument, but it also was a sadly deteriorating relic. Peter Romeo, a local artisan-craftsman and Sheepshead Bay enthusiast, enlisted a bunch of talented teenagers to paint panels that covered the entrances with scenes of past Lundy's splendor. This cosmetic effort had a heartening effect of fostering community pride in and respect for this great building. Perhaps if enough attention was paid to its plight, someone would really bring it back to life.

It wasn't the derelict old Lundy's building Frank Cretella had in mind for his Sheepshead Bay restaurant in early 1995. He had thought of taking over a spot some few blocks to the east along Emmons. But he kept getting warnings that Lundy's was going to reopen—in fact, a sign appeared on the building—and if that happened, then it would be killing competition for any other seafood restaurant in the area. This wasn't the old days when the area could support a seemingly endless number of eateries.

He knew the restaurant and its lore. It had been a favorite of his Brooklyn uncle, Patsy Cretella, and over the years he had taken the unofficial tour given by longtime caretaker Raul Badillo, who would guide the curious through the piled-up chairs, the fully equipped kitchens, by the tattered draperies and the water-stained walls. It was all there, as slowly crumbling as the *Titanic* underwater and as easily recognizable. Frank went to take another look at this possible competition—by then everything had been sold. All that remained of the old Lundy's was the darkened stucco walls, the old clam bar, the wrought-iron railings of the stairway. He immediately realized that this was the space that would give him the freedom to create the kind of restaurant he wanted.

Frank canceled his other deal and determined to take the lease for this restaurant. The entire block-long two-story restaurant would be impossible. In this day and age you couldn't fill it. The kitchens would be inadequate because of the increased number of menu items. What was decided on was 42 percent of the old space, including the old kitchens and the second floor, which would be used for special events.

Like Irving Lundy, Frank Cretella was a precocious entrepreneur. At sixteen, before he got his driver's license, he had already started a towing service. But what fascinated him was the food business. And like the early century Lundys, his business operations would be family affairs. With his fiancée, Jeanne (whom he married

The Rockaway Ferry to Breezy Point and Rockaway Point, the Sheepshead Bay dock with the Frederick Lundy *ferry, 1948. A day's excursion would be the ferry trip to the Rockaways, capped by dinner at Lundy's. Photograph by John D. Morrell. Collection of The Brooklyn Historical Association.*

in 1982), he managed to obtain a concession at the Staten Island Zoo, a concession for which their mothers and aunts cooked in their home kitchens. In the early morning hours, the food would be piled into a van and carted off to the zoo. At one time the number of extended family cooks came to twenty. When Frank went to look at a concession site in Central Park it was only the second time he had been in Manhattan by himself. He was thrilled by the vitality of Central Park life: Rollerbladers, hordes sunning themselves in the Sheep Meadow, the cyclists crowding the roadway, runners breaking out of their lane. The concession he got was the Mineral Springs Pavilion near Tavern on the Green at the southern end of the park, and he turned it into a health food stand—with mothers and aunts trying their hands at organic muffins and combinations of carrot, parsley, orange, and ginger juices. The success of the Pavilion encouraged the Parks Department to ask them to take over the concession at the Boat House—it had just been padlocked by the IRS because of the default of the previous concessionaire.

The family was called in again. Overnight they scraped and painted, reworked and scrubbed the counter space, and decorated with giant kites this new space, and within twenty-four hours, Frank and Jeanne were ready to open. When renewal time came, Frank proposed that the unused storage shed and open area be turned into a lakeside restaurant with catering space. That notion was rewarded with the grant of a long-term lease. Their first restaurant, The Boathouse in Central Park, was opened in 1985. With it, Frank and Jeanne created a multimillion-dollar success. But they learned how to run a restaurant by making every mistake in the book: overstaffing, an unqualified staff, a complicated menu, figuring out how to deal with reservations for a restaurant off a park path, making evening diners feel safe. What it did was make them feel somewhat secure about opening a restaurant on the scale of Lundy's.

The model for the new Lundy's was the Chicago restaurant Scoozi's: there would be an open kitchen with a wood-burning oven, comfortable banquettes, diverse and discrete areas—all these were not features of the old Lundy's. But the stucco walls, lightened up and minus the ground clam shells, would remain, and so would hints of the original light fixtures in the design of the new ones. The menu would include the Shore Dinner (still the most popular choice), but there would be daily specials dependent on what the market had avail-

Lundy's reborn, front dining room, 1996. Courtesy of the Tam Corporation.

able. Sure, there would be the groans that this was not the Lundy's of old, but this new Lundy's had to appeal to a new audience. The continuity is in the location, the preserved exterior, and the sense that this place is based on a relation to the pleasures and aspirations of the people of Brooklyn. The old-timers returned, driving to Brooklyn from Long Island, New Jersey, and Connecticut, and then there were the new patrons, feeling they were visiting a historical site. Some were happy, some thought too much had been altered, and some wondered why the Shore Dinner no longer cost $4.95. Lundy's was there, but it wasn't exactly the same. It never is.

Many who are returning to the restaurant after many, many years begin to cry when they remember what the old days were like. It stands for vanished youth, family bonds, happier times. Before patrons order, they ask for the manager, Steve Gattulo, to show him where their table was in the old days, to talk of clams thirty cents a dozen, to recall the waiter who was their friend. But Lundy's is once again a place for celebration, for the vibrant feel of a vital community, for having your first clam and cracking your first lobster.

For those of us who make periodic sentimental returns to Brooklyn, there is gratitude that one institution has been revived, that so wonderful a feature of our past has not been discarded, that we can show our children where our parents took us on Sundays. We want things to remain, even allowing for modification and change. In Brooklyn, we were nurtured by ballparks, active street life, restaurants, schools. Lundy's then was a statement of the bounty of life, in food and vibrant community. Why we treasure this restaurant and why we treasure the memory of Brooklyn, is because the community welcomed us, served us, encouraged us, and nurtured us. We like being reminded that where we were brought up infused us with the expectation of life's being marvelously generous.

Lundy's, stairway to mid-level, 1996. The wrought-iron railings in the foreground are from the original Lundy's. Note also the original terrazzo marble steps. Courtesy of the Tam Corporation.

The
Recipes

A Note About the Recipes

The recipes on the following pages represent a mix of the old-style Lundy's and the new Lundy's. Unfortunately, the original recipes from the old Lundy's were not made available to us. So to re-create the flavors of that time, I spent many hours researching old Lundy's menus and seafood books of the era, as well as interviewing old customers. What we offer here are the highlights of the original Lundy's menu—the incomparable, flaky biscuits, the thick seafood chowders, perfectly broiled fish, crispy fried clams, steamers, stuffed clams, and lobster. You'll rediscover classics like Lobster Newburg, Oysters Rockefeller, Broiled Stuffed Lobster, Oyster Stew, Creamed Spinach, and Hash Brown Potatoes. Many of these old favorites are laden with butter and cream. They have been lightened somewhat in an effort to appeal to modern tastes.

The majority of the recipes representing Lundy's today were developed by Neil Kleinberg, the original chef of the new Lundy's. You might call them new-wave Lundy's—recipes like Crispy Skin Salmon with Horseradish Mashed Potatoes and Balsamic Glaze; Whole Roasted Fish with Potatoes, Fennel, and Shallots; or Fennel-and-Pepper-Crusted Tuna with Spinach and Orange-Campari Butter Sauce. I have adapted Kleinberg's wonderful combinations so they can be easily prepared at home.

—Kathy Gunst

7

Soups and Broth

New England Clam Chowder

Lundy's Brooklyn Red (or Manhattan Clam Chowder)

Crab and Lobster Bisque

Oyster Stew

New England Clam Chowder

SERVES 8

This is a particularly rich chowder, chock-full of potatoes, clams, and onions. If you make the chowder a day ahead of time, the flavors will really come together.

> 5 pounds quahog (chowder clams), or 7 pounds
>   cherrystone clams
> 3 strips bacon
> 2 tablespoons butter
> 1 large onion, cut into large dice
> 6 medium-large potatoes, peeled and cut into large
>   dice
> 1 bay leaf
> 5½ tablespoons flour
> 2 cups heavy cream
> 2 cups milk
> Salt
> Freshly ground black pepper

Scrub the clams clean and place them in a large stockpot with 8 cups water. Bring to a boil and let steam for about 8 minutes, or until the clams open. Strain the clam water and set aside. Remove the clams from the shell and chop coarsely. Reserve the chopped clam meat and discard the shells.

Clean any sand from the bottom of the pot. Cook the bacon over moderate heat until just crispy, being careful not to let it, or the fat, burn. Remove the bacon and reserve. Add the butter and the onion and sauté for about 3 minutes, stirring frequently, being careful not to let them burn. Add the potatoes and the bay leaf and stir well. Add the flour and stir. Add the clam water, making sure not to add any sand that may have settled at the bottom, and let simmer 15 minutes. Stir in the cream and milk and bring to a vigorous simmer over moderately high heat. Reduce the heat to a gentle simmer, add the clam meat, and cook for about 10 minutes, or until thickened and flavorful and the potatoes are tender. Taste for seasoning and add salt and pepper as needed.

Lundy's Brooklyn Red (or Manhattan Clam Chowder)

SERVES 8

Like all chowders, this one tastes better made a day ahead of time. This is a classic that combines clams, fresh clam broth, tomatoes, potatoes, vegetables, and herbs.

4 pounds quahog, or 6 pounds cherrystone clams

2 tablespoons butter

2 large or 3 medium onions, cut into large dice

2 carrots, cut into large dice

2 stalks celery, cut into large dice

2 cloves garlic, minced

1 bay leaf

3 medium potatoes, peeled and cut into large dice

One 28-ounce can whole peeled tomatoes

1 teaspoon tomato paste

1½ teaspoons dry thyme

1½ teaspoons dry oregano
Freshly ground black pepper
Salt (optional)

Scrub the clams well to remove any external debris. Place the clams in a large pot with 8 cups water. Place over high heat and bring to a boil. Reduce the heat and cook until the clams *just* open, about 5 minutes. Remove from the heat and strain the broth into a large bowl and set aside. Separate the clams from their shells. Coarsely chop the clams and set aside; discard the shells.

Clean any sand from the bottom of the pot. Heat the butter over a moderately low heat. Add the onions and cook, stirring frequently to prevent browning, about 8 minutes, or until soft. Add the carrots, celery, garlic, bay leaf, potatoes, tomatoes, tomato paste, thyme, oregano, and pepper, and stir to mix. Add the reserved clam broth into the pot and bring to a boil over high heat. Reduce the heat to moderate and cook, uncovered, for 30 to 40 minutes. Add the clams and cook another 10 minutes, or until the potatoes are tender. Taste for seasoning and serve piping hot.

111

Crab and Lobster Bisque

SERVES 14

This is a serious recipe for serious soup lovers. Plan on spending at least three hours in the kitchen and then settle in to feast on one of the richest, most sublime bisques imaginable.

Here's how the recipe goes: the shellfish (you can use crab and/or lobster) is seared over high heat and then cooked with an assortment of vegetables. The fish is flamed with brandy, and then white wine and tomatoes are added and cooked down to an essence. Clam broth or water, herbs, and seasonings are added, and the bisque continues to cook. Meanwhile you make a roux in a separate pan and whisk it into the broth. The bisque is then strained through a colander, and then the fun begins: the crabs and lobster are pounded and smashed into the colander so that all the juices and flavors are released into the broth. The bisque is finally reduced with heavy cream, strained again, and the feasting begins.

Don't be scared off by the number of steps involved; I guarantee you the effort will be well rewarded. Because the bisque is labor-intensive, be sure to make a large batch. There's enough here to serve at least fourteen people; invite a crowd or freeze the bisque in batches and save for a cold, wintry day.

6 pounds live hard-shell crabs, or 3 pounds live crab
    and 3 pounds live lobster, or any combination you
    like
¼ cup plus 2 tablespoons olive oil
2 medium onions, diced
4 carrots, diced
4 stalks celery, diced
10 to 12 cloves garlic, crushed with the side of a knife
1 large leek, thinly sliced
1 cup brandy
4 cups dry white wine
Two 28-ounce cans peeled plum tomatoes (7 cups)
4 ounces tomato paste (½ cup)
2 bay leaves
4 sprigs fresh thyme

4 sprigs fresh tarragon
1 cup coarsely chopped parsley
1 tablespoon white or black peppercorns
2 pinches saffron (optional)
12 cups clam stock or water or a combination
½ pound butter
1 cup flour
2 cups heavy cream
Salt
Freshly ground black pepper

With a heavy cleaver or a large, sharp knife, hold the crabs on a work surface shell side down and split them in half to kill. Place the crab in a large bowl and drain off all the juices that settle in the bowl. For lobsters: hold the lobster on a work surface shell side down and split in half lengthwise down the middle. Remove the tail and claws and place in a bowl. Remove the sac from the lobster and discard; place the body in the bowl. Remove the rubber bands holding the claws together on both the crabs and lobster and discard.

In a large, heavy-bottomed stockpot, heat the ¼ cup oil over high heat until smoking hot. Add the crab and lobster, shell side down, and sauté 10 minutes, stirring occasionally to ensure that the shellfish cooks on both sides. Still working over high heat, add the onions, carrots, celery, garlic, leek, and the remaining 2 tablespoons oil and cook, stirring occasionally, for 10 minutes, or until the vegetables start to soften. Be careful not to let the vegetables brown.

Add the brandy and light the mixture with a match and let it burn down. (The flame will die out naturally when the alcohol evaporates.) Add the white wine, plum tomatoes, tomato paste, bay

113

leaves, thyme, tarragon, parsley, peppercorns, and saffron and let cook, over high heat, for about 40 minutes, or until the mixture is cooked down and there is *almost* no liquid remaining. Keep stirring the bottom of the pot to avoid sticking. Add the clam stock and bring to a boil. When the stock boils, skim off any foam that rises to the surface. Let simmer over moderately low heat while making the roux.

In a medium saucepan, melt the butter over moderate heat. Stir in the flour and let cook about 3 minutes. Using a whisk, stir a cup of the hot broth into the roux and mix well to avoid any lumps. Add the roux/stock to the large pot of stock and mix well to avoid lumps. Reduce the heat to low and cook 15 minutes, skimming off any foam that rises to the surface.

Remove several crab claws and/or the lobster tail and claws at this point and reserve for garnish.

Place a large colander over another stockpot or large pot. Pour the bisque through the colander. Using a large mortar, mallet, or the back of a small pot, smash the crab and/or lobster shells and vegetables through the colander. Make sure to crush the shells as well as possible to get as much of the juice, pulp, and vegetables that may be stuck inside the shells. Discard the remaining shells and vegetables in the colander. (The bisque can be made 24 hours ahead of time up to this point.)

Heat the bisque over a moderately high heat and add the cream. Let the bisque simmer vigorously and season with salt and pepper. The bisque can be served as is or strained one last time through a strainer lined with cheesecloth to catch the rest of the impurities left after the first straining.

Remove the meat from the reserved crab and/or lobster shells and chop coarsely. Serve the hot bisque garnished with a generous tablespoon of the crab and/or lobster meat.

Oyster Stew

SERVES 8

This is one of the simplest, most delicious stews imaginable. Fresh oysters (or soft-shell clams) are briefly sautéed in butter and then mixed with piping hot cream, milk, and natural oyster juices. Serve with oyster crackers or biscuits.

> 48 fresh oysters or soft-shell clams, shucked with the
>   juices reserved (about 1½ pounds shelled)
> 4 cups milk
> 4 cups heavy cream
> 4 tablespoons butter
> Dash of Worcestershire sauce (optional)
> Salt
> Freshly ground black pepper
> Sweet paprika

115

Separate the oysters or clams from the juices and reserve.

In a large, heavy-bottomed saucepan, or 2 medium saucepans, heat the milk and cream; add the oyster or clam juices. Cook over moderate heat for 8 minutes, or until slightly thickened and somewhat reduced.

In a medium skillet, heat the butter over moderate heat. Add the oysters or clams and a very small dash of Worcestershire sauce if desired. (There are two schools of thinking on the addition of this sauce: some purists, myself included, don't think this stew needs any seasoning other than salt and pepper. Others like the rich, slightly smoky flavor the Worcestershire lends.) Sauté for 1 minute and remove from the heat and add to the hot milk-cream mixture. Season with salt and pepper and heat through for about 2 minutes. Serve in large soup bowls or soup plates and garnish with a dash of paprika.

8

Appetizers

Steamers (Steamed Soft-Shell Clams)

Mussels Steamed with Shallots and White Wine

Clams Oreganata

Lundy's Crab Cakes

Oysters on the Half Shell with Two Sauces

Oysters Rockefeller

Seafood Fritters

Shrimp Cocktail

Seafood Salad

Steamers (Steamed Soft-Shell Clams)

SERVES 4 AS AN APPETIZER

This is a standard part of any clambake and has been on the menus at Lundy's since the early days. Steamed clams are traditionally served with the natural clam broth and melted butter.

> 2 pounds steamer clams (soft-shell clams)
> ¼ cup cold water
> About 6 tablespoons butter, melted
> Freshly ground black pepper

Wash the clams well in several changes of cold water to remove any sand or dirt clinging to the shells. Place the clams in a large pot with the ¼ cup water and place them over high heat. Steam for about 4 to 6 minutes, depending on the size, or until the shells open. Serve with melted butter and pour the clam broth from the pot into mugs with a grinding of pepper.

To eat: remove the clam from the shell and remove the skin off the neck of the clams. Dip the clams in the hot broth to remove any excess sand and then into the melted butter. The hot broth, with a grinding of pepper, is delicious to drink; beware of the sand that accumulates at the bottom of the mug.

Mussels Steamed
with Shallots and White Wine

SERVES 4 AS AN APPETIZER

Serve these mussels with warm crusty bread or biscuits. They are also delicious served on top of linguine.

1 tablespoon olive oil
¼ cup chopped shallots
3 cloves garlic, minced
2 pounds cleaned mussels
1 cup dry white wine
½ cup minced fresh parsley

118

Heat the oil over moderate heat in a large pot. Add the shallots and half the garlic and sauté for 3 minutes, stirring frequently to prevent burning. Raise the heat to high and add the mussels. Stir well to coat them thoroughly and add the remaining garlic and wine. Cook for 4 to 6 minutes, or until the mussels are opened. Sprinkle the mussels with the parsley and divide in serving bowls.

Clams Oreganata

SERVES 4

These tasty morsels are ideal for a party because they can be prepared ahead of time (covered and refrigerated) and popped in the oven at the last minute.

> 12 littleneck clams
> About ½ cup oreganata mix (page 173)
> Olive oil
> 1 lemon, cut into wedges
> Parsley sprigs for garnish (optional)

Preheat the oven to 400 degrees.

Shuck the clams and place the clams on the half shell in a shallow roasting pan or pie plate, reserving the clam juice. Sprinkle a generous teaspoon of oreganata mix on top of each clam; don't pack it down but simply mound it over the clam. Dab the top of each clam with just a touch of olive oil (using either a pastry brush or spoon). Pour half of the clam juice around, not on top of, the clams.

Bake the clams for 10 minutes, or until golden brown. Accompany the clams with the lemon wedges and a parsley sprig, if desired.

Lundy's Crab Cakes

MAKES ABOUT 12 SMALL CRAB CAKES,
6 APPETIZER SERVINGS OR 4 MAIN COURSE SERVINGS

Serve these moist, colorful crab cakes with Lundy's tartar sauce (page 172) and lemon wedges.

1½ tablespoons olive oil
½ red pepper, chopped into small dice
¼ yellow pepper, chopped into small dice
¼ green pepper, chopped into small dice
¼ red onion, chopped into small dice
½ scallion, finely chopped
1 tablespoon chopped parsley
Salt
Freshly ground black pepper
2 tablespoons mayonnaise
1 teaspoon Dijon mustard
¾ teaspoon Worcestershire sauce
Dash Tabasco or to taste
½ teaspoon lemon juice
½ pound crabmeat (lump or backfin), picked through
     to remove cartilage and shells
About 4 ounces bread crumbs, fresh or dried
1 to 2 tablespoons vegetable oil for cooking
Lemon wedges
Tartar sauce

Heat the oil in a medium skillet over moderate heat. Add the peppers, onion, scallion, and parsley and sauté, stirring frequently, for 5 to 6 minutes, or until the vegetables are softened but not browned. Season with salt and pepper and set aside to cool.

In a large bowl, mix the mayonnaise, mustard, Worcestershire sauce, Tabasco, and lemon juice. Add the crabmeat and sautéed vegetables, and adjust seasoning with salt and pepper. Add enough bread crumbs to bind the mixture. (The recipe can be made ahead of time to this point and refrigerated for several hours.)

Form the mixture into 2- to 2½-inch patties. Heat about 1 tablespoon of the vegetable oil in a large skillet over a moderately high heat. Add the crab cakes and sauté 3 to 4 minutes on each side, or until golden brown and cooked through, adding additional oil if needed. Drain on paper towels and serve with lemon wedges and tartar sauce.

Oysters on the Half Shell with Two Sauces

SERVES 4

Briny and fresh raw oysters are served on the half shell with a peppery mignonette sauce and a horseradish-spiked cocktail sauce. Be sure to accompany with a bowl of oyster crackers and lemon wedges.

> 12 fresh oysters, opened on the half shell
> Mignonette sauce (page 171)
> Lundy's cocktail sauce (page 173)
> 1 lemon, cut into wedges

Open the oysters and place on a bed of crushed ice. Serve with the mignonette sauce, cocktail sauce, and lemon wedges on the side.

Oysters Rockefeller

SERVES 4

A true classic, this recipe has many variations, but all of them call for spinach as a topping for fresh oysters. In this rendition, oysters are baked on a bed of rock or coarse kosher salt and topped with a creamy tarragon-spiked spinach mixture and a sprinkling of fresh bread crumbs. They are rich and thoroughly addictive.

> 1 tablespoon olive oil or butter
>
> 2 shallots, chopped
>
> 10 ounces fresh spinach, stemmed, well washed and
>   dried, about 8 packed cups
>
> 1½ tablespoons chopped fresh tarragon
>
> Salt
>
> Freshly ground black pepper
>
> ¾ cup heavy cream
>
> 12 fresh oysters
>
> 2 to 3 cups coarse kosher or rock salt
>
> About ¼ cup fresh bread crumbs
>
> 2 tablespoons butter, cut into 12 small cubes

In a large skillet, heat the oil over moderate heat. Add the shallots and sauté about 3 minutes. Add the spinach and, stirring frequently, cook about 10 minutes, or until softened. Add half the tarragon and salt and pepper to taste. Let cool slightly before coarsely chopping the mixture.

Return the spinach to the skillet and heat over moderately high heat. Add the cream and let cook until the cream is slightly thickened, about 5 minutes. Add the remaining tarragon and adjust the seasoning. (The recipe can be made several hours ahead of time up to this point.)

Using a shucking knife, carefully open the oysters, leaving them on the half shell. Pour the salt in a medium-size shallow roasting pan or baking sheet and place the oysters on top. Divide the spinach mixture by adding a generous tablespoon to the top of each oyster. Top each oyster with some bread crumbs and a cube of butter.

Preheat the broiler. Broil the oysters for 3 to 4 minutes, or until the topping is hot and the bread crumbs are golden brown. Serve immediately.

Seafood Fritters

SERVES 8 AS AN APPETIZER OR 4 AS A MAIN COURSE

My mouth waters just thinking about these light, juicy fritters chock-full of shrimp, clams, and potatoes. This is a great dish to make when you have leftover shrimp or potatoes. Don't be turned off by the idea of deep-frying at home. If you get the oil hot enough, these fritters won't be the least bit greasy.

Serve the fritters as an hors d'oeuvre, first course, or lunch dish. You can make these fritters using any combination of seafood—try a crab and clam fritter or a mussel and clam fritter. You want a total of 1 cup cooked seafood and ½ cup cooked potato.

Serve with the Spicy Mayonnaise sauce on page 171.

6 littleneck or 4 cherrystone clams
6 to 8 medium-size shrimp

1 medium potato, cut into dice

¾ cup flour

½ teaspoon baking powder

½ teaspoon salt

¼ teaspoon white pepper

½ cup half and half

1 egg

½ cup finely diced onions

1 clove garlic, minced (optional)

1 tablespoon minced fresh chives

½ tablespoon Tabasco or hot pepper sauce

½ tablespoon Worcestershire sauce

½ tablespoon olive oil

Vegetable oil for frying

Spicy Mayonnaise

Place the clams in a medium pot and add ½ cup water. Bring to a boil and simmer until the clams *just* open. Remove the clams from the shells and coarsely chop; set aside and discard shells.

Add the shrimp to the clam broth in the pot and simmer over moderate heat until the shrimp turn pink, about 4 minutes. Drain the shrimp from the pot and let cool slightly. Peel the shrimp and coarsely chop; set aside. Reserve or freeze the broth for making chowder or fish stock.

Place the potato in a medium pot and add 2 inches of cold water. Bring to a boil and simmer until just tender, about 4 minutes. Drain and set aside. (The recipe can be done up to this point 2 days ahead of time.)

In a large bowl, mix together the flour, baking powder, salt, and pepper. Measure out the half and half in a glass measuring cup and add the egg and whisk lightly. Add the half and half and egg mixture to the flour, along with the onions, garlic, chives, Tabasco, and Worcestershire and gently fold the mixture together. Add the olive oil. (The mixture can be made several hours ahead of time; cover and refrigerate until ready to fry.)

Fill a deep skillet, wok, or deep fryer with at least 2½ inches of oil and heat over a high heat until it reaches 350 degrees. (Test the oil temperature with a deep-fry thermometer or a candy thermometer.)

Use 2 tablespoons of batter to form each fritter. When the oil is hot, form each fritter and add to the hot oil. Cook for 2 to 2½ minutes on each side, or until golden brown and cooked through. Drain on paper towels. Experiment with the first fritter to see how long it needs to cook through; be careful not to let it burn. Serve hot or warm with the spicy mayonnaise. The fritters can be reheated in a low 250-degree oven until warmed through, about 6 minutes, but they taste best served immediately.

125

Shrimp Cocktail

SERVES 4

Although precooked shrimp are available in most grocery and fish stores, this shrimp cocktail has a superior flavor when you cook the shrimp fresh in a court bouillon and serve them with Lundy's cocktail sauce.

4 cups court bouillon (page 174)
1 pound medium-size shrimp

Lundy's cocktail sauce (page 173)
1 lemon, cut into wedges

Bring the court bouillon to a rapid simmer over moderately high heat. Add the shrimp and let cook about 3 minutes, or until the shell is pink and the shrimp is cooked through. Remove with a slotted spoon and let cool. Peel, devein, and chill the shrimp before serving. Serve with cocktail sauce and lemon wedges on the side.

Seafood Salad

SERVES 6 AS AN APPETIZER OR 4 AS A MAIN COURSE

Shrimp, scallops, and calamari are combined with crunchy bits of colorful sweet peppers, red onion, celery, capers, and parsley in a citrus-flavored vinaigrette. Serve this fresh-tasting salad over a bed of lettuce or in a "cone" of radicchio accompanied by warm biscuits or a crunchy loaf of bread.

3 cups court bouillon (page 174)
½ pound medium-size shrimp
½ pound medium-size sea scallops (about 18 to 20)
1½ pounds cleaned calamari, fresh or frozen
¼ medium red onion, diced
½ cup red pepper, cut into large dice
½ cup yellow pepper, cut into large dice
½ cup green pepper, cut into large dice
1 stalk celery, cut into large dice
¼ cup minced fresh parsley

1½ tablespoons capers, coarsely chopped
2 cloves garlic, minced
⅛ teaspoon crushed red pepper
¼ teaspoon oregano (optional)
¼ cup lemon juice
Peel of ½ lemon, julienned
1 tablespoon lime juice
⅓ cup olive oil
Salt
Freshly ground black pepper
Mixture of greens

In a stockpot, bring the court bouillon to a boil over high heat. Add the shrimp and let cook for 3 minutes. Remove with a slotted spoon and let cool. Peel and devein the shrimp, and cut in half. Place in a large salad bowl.

Place the scallops in the boiling court bouillon and cook for 2½ to 3 minutes, or until cooked through. Remove with a slotted spoon and let cool. Cut in half, or quarters if they are large, and place in the large bowl.

Put the calamari in the boiling court bouillon for 3 to 5 minutes, or until cooked through but still tender. Remove with a slotted spoon and let cool. Cut into bite-size slices and place in the large bowl.

Add the onion, peppers, celery, parsley, capers, garlic, red pepper, and oregano and mix well with the seafood. Add the lemon juice, lemon peel, lime juice, and oil and mix well. Season to taste with the salt and pepper. Serve cold or at room temperature on a bed of lettuce.

9

Seafood Main Courses

Steamed Lobster

Broiled Stuffed Lobster

Lobster Newburg

Angry Lobster (Roasted Lobster
with Garlic, Basil, and
Crushed Red Pepper)

Lobster Salad

Lobster Eggs Benedict

Sautéed Soft-Shell Crabs
with Brown Almond Butter

Fried Clams

Linguine with Clam Sauce

Penne with Grilled Shrimp

Shrimp Jambalaya

Shrimp Scampi

Broiled Fish

Pan-Fried Flounder with
Brown Butter and Almonds

Baked Bluefish with Basil,
Tomatoes, and Onions

Crispy Skin Atlantic Salmon
with Horseradish Mashed Potatoes
and Balsamic Glaze

Salmon with Cornmeal Crust
and Almond-Caper Butter

Fennel-and-Pepper-Crusted Tuna
with Spinach and Orange-
Campari Butter Sauce

Whole Roasted Fish with
Potatoes, Fennel, and Shallots

Roasted Fish Mediterranean Style

Steamed Lobster

Steaming, versus boiling, produces the tenderest, moistest lobster imaginable. Fill a large pot with 3 to 4 inches of water and a sprinkle of salt and bring to a boil. (If you have access to fresh seaweed, add a few strips instead of the salt for a fresh, briny flavor.) Add the lobsters to the pot *shell side down* so all the juices get caught in the shell and are not lost in the pot. Cover and let steam for about 10 minutes for a 1-pound lobster and up to 20 minutes for a 2-pounder. To test for doneness, simply pull off one of the legs; if it pulls off easily, the lobster is ready. Drain the lobster and serve hot with plenty of melted butter, lemon wedges, and hot pepper sauce if desired. If you're using the lobster meat for another dish, let it cool before cutting the shell open and removing the meat.

129

Broiled Stuffed Lobster

SERVES 4

Although Lundy's serves lobster broiled with a rich seafood stuffing, this version is lighter and simpler. The lobsters are steamed until almost cooked, split down the middle, and filled with an oreganata bread crumb mixture and broiled until hot and crusty. You can pre-steam the lobsters and finish them off just before serving, which makes this an ideal dish for a dinner party.

Four 1½-pound lobsters
Several strips fresh seaweed (see Note)

2 cups oreganata mix (page 173)
4 tablespoons butter, cut into small cubes
1 lemon, cut into wedges

Fill a large pot with 2 to 3 inches of water and bring to a boil.
Add the seaweed if available. Steam the lobsters, placing them in
the pot shell side down, and cook 7 minutes. Remove from the pot
and let cool. (The lobsters can be made several hours ahead of time
up to this point. Cover and refrigerate until ready to proceed.)

Preheat the broiler.

Place the lobsters on a clean work surface shell side down.
Using a large, sharp knife, split them down the center and remove
the sac located at the top of the lobster body. Place the lobsters on
a shallow broiler pan and remove the rubber bands on the claws.
Place ½ cup of the oreganata mix into each lobster body and tail,
pressing down so the stuffing stays within the shell. Top each
lobster with 1 tablespoon butter. Pour ½ cup water *around*, not on
top of, the lobsters.

Place the lobster pan at least 3 inches below the broiler (if it
gets too close the stuffing will burn before the lobster is cooked
through) and broil about 5 minutes, or until cooked through and
the stuffing is hot. Serve hot accompanied by the lemon wedges.

NOTE: Gather the seaweed on a beach or ask for it at your local fish
store.

Lobster Newburg

SERVES 4

This is one of those incredibly rich, cream-filled dishes that was popular back in the early days of Lundy's. The sauce—butter, dry sherry, cream, and egg yolks—is made in a double boiler, and cooked lobster meat is folded into the sauce. Traditionally Lobster Newburg is served on toast points or steamed white rice. I've found that by serving the dish in a gratin dish and placing it under the broiler for a few minutes, the Newburg takes on a golden crust that adds a wonderful texture and causes the flavors to really come together.

2 tablespoons butter
¼ cup good quality dry sherry
3 egg yolks
¾ cup heavy cream
Salt
Freshly ground black pepper
Dash of Tabasco or hot pepper sauce (optional)
2 cups cooked lobster meat, cut into bite-size pieces
    (from two 1¼-pound lobsters)
Tomalley and roe from lobster (optional)
Sweet paprika
Cooked white rice or toast points

In the top of a double boiler set over gently simmering water, melt the butter. Add the sherry and let simmer 3 minutes.

In a small bowl, whisk together the egg yolks and cream. Slowly whisk the yolk-cream mixture into the butter mixture until thick enough to coat the back of a spoon, about 10 minutes. Add a touch of salt, pepper, and Tabasco if desired. Gently stir in the lobster meat and tomalley and roe if desired and taste for seasoning. Let heat through for about a minute. The Newburg can be served at this point on top of rice or toast points and sprinkled with paprika.

Alternately, preheat the broiler. Place the Newburg in a small gratin dish and sprinkle with paprika. Broil for 3 to 5 minutes, or until a golden brown "crust" appears on top. Serve on rice or toast points.

Angry Lobster (Roasted Lobster with Garlic, Basil, and Crushed Red Pepper)

SERVES 4 GENEROUS PORTIONS

A live lobster is chopped into bite-size pieces, tossed with olive oil, garlic, basil, rosemary, and crushed red pepper and roasted in a hot oven until tender and juicy. This is a very unconventional way to prepare lobster, but once you've tried it you may never steam or boil a lobster again. Serve with pasta (tossed with marinara sauce or olive oil and sautéed garlic) or rice, and with garlic bread for mopping up the juices at the bottom of the plate.

> 4 live lobsters (about 1 pound each)
> Coarse kosher salt
> Freshly ground black pepper
> ¼ cup good quality olive oil
> 8 large cloves garlic, peeled and sliced
> 1 cup fresh basil, torn into large pieces
> 2 to 3 sprigs fresh rosemary, cut into 2-inch pieces
>   (twig and herb)
> About 1 teaspoon crushed red pepper

Preheat the oven to 450 degrees. Place a large, shallow roasting pan in the hot oven and preheat it for 5 to 10 minutes, or until very hot.

Place the live lobsters on a work surface shell side up facing toward you. Using a large, sharp knife, make an incision where the tail and the body connect, with the blade facing the head of the lobster. Push down on the knife, cutting the body in two. (This will kill the lobster.) Using your hands, twist the tail off and pull off the claws. Separate the body into halves, then cut into quarters, slicing across the body. Remove and discard the sac at the top of the head. Remove the tomalley and set aside.

Cut the tail across into four pieces. Separate the knuckle from the claw. With a quick action, use the back of the knife to crack the top of the claw. Turn the knife over and cut the claw in half at the joint. Make a small incision in the soft bottom part of the knuckle and cut in half. At the end of this process you should have 16 pieces of lobster. Repeat with the remaining lobsters.

Place the lobster pieces in a large bowl and season with salt and pepper.

Remove the preheated pan from the oven and carefully add the oil to the pan. (The oil will smoke and splatter.) Place the lobster pieces in the hot pan, shell side down, and roast 6 minutes, or until the shells are red. Sprinkle the garlic, basil, rosemary, and crushed red pepper on top (try to get the garlic cloves to stick to the bottom of the pan so they'll brown) and roast another 6 minutes, or until the lobster is cooked through but still tender; it will continue to cook once it's removed from the oven. Remove from the oven and serve hot.

Lobster Salad

SERVES 4

If you cook the lobster meat ahead of time, this dish can be assembled at the last minute. Serve with buttered toast triangles, warm biscuits (page 164), or in a warm hot dog roll accompanied by buttery, tender lettuce leaves.

> ¼ cup mayonnaise, bottled or homemade
> 3 tablespoons capers, drained
> 2 tablespoons fresh lemon juice
> Freshly ground black pepper
> 1½ cups cooked lobster meat, chopped (from two
>   1¼-pound lobsters)
> 1 cup celery, thinly sliced

134

In a medium bowl, gently mix the mayonnaise, capers, lemon juice, and pepper. Gently mix in the lobster meat and celery.

Lobster Eggs Benedict

SERVES 4 TO 8

A rich, luscious dish ideal for brunch or lunch.

> 8 large eggs plus 4 egg yolks
> 1½ tablespoons white wine vinegar
> 1 teaspoon fresh lemon juice

⅛ teaspoon cayenne pepper

1½ teaspoons salt

1 cup sweet butter, melted

1 cup cooked lobster meat, coarsely chopped, from
　　one 1½-pound lobster

2 tablespoons olive oil

20 ounces fresh spinach, washed and stemmed

Salt

Pepper

4 Lundy's ultimate biscuits (page 164) or English
　　muffins

2 tomatoes, diced

1 tablespoon chopped fresh chives

Using a whisk, beat the 4 egg yolks, 1 tablespoon of the
vinegar, lemon juice, 2 tablespoons water, cayenne, and ½ teaspoon
of the salt in a large, nonreactive bowl. Place the bowl over a large
saucepan of simmering water, or on the top of a double boiler, and
continue whisking until the mixture becomes thick and coats the
back of a spoon. Gradually add the butter and whisk until all the
butter is incorporated. Add the lobster meat and keep in a warm
place so the sauce won't curdle or separate.

Heat the olive oil over moderately high heat in a large
saucepan. Add the spinach, working in batches, and cook, stirring
frequently, until just wilted, 3 to 5 minutes. Season with salt and
pepper. Keep warm in the pan over very low heat.

In a large saucepan, simmer 2 to 3 quarts of water. Add the
remaining vinegar and salt to the water and carefully crack the
whole eggs into the water. Poach about 1½ minutes, until the eggs
are set but the yolk is still slightly runny. Carefully remove the eggs
with a slotted spoon and drain on paper towels. Keep warm.

Split the biscuits in half. Place a few leaves of cooked spinach on top of each biscuit half, top with a poached egg, and spoon the lobster hollandaise over the top. Garnish with tomatoes, chives, and more spinach.

Sautéed Soft-Shell Crabs with Brown Almond Butter

SERVES 4

You can find this specialty in late spring when crabs are molting. This is a simple preparation that makes the most of the crabs' fresh, juicy flavor. You can also simply sauté the crabs and serve them as a sandwich with tartar sauce on biscuits or crusty French bread.

About ¾ cup flour
Salt
Freshly ground black pepper
3 tablespoons butter
1½ tablespoons olive oil
8 large soft-shell crabs, cleaned
¾ cup slivered almonds
4 tablespoons lemon juice
2 lemons, cut into wedges

Place the flour on a plate and season liberally with salt and pepper. Working in two large skillets, heat 1 tablespoon of the butter and ½ tablespoon of the oil in each pan over a moderately high heat. Dredge the crabs in the seasoned flour, making sure both sides are covered. Sauté the crabs in the hot fat for 3 minutes on each side, or until golden brown. Remove the crabs from the skillet and place on warm plates.

Add the remaining butter and oil to the skillet and heat for 1 minute. Add the almonds and sauté about 2 minutes, or until golden brown. Add the lemon juice and salt and pepper, scatter the sautéed nuts over the crabs, and surround with the lemon wedges.

Fried Clams

SERVES 4

Fried clams feature prominently in many people's memories of meals at the old Lundy's—crispy and crunchy on the outside with a soft, melt-in-your-mouth clam belly inside. Deep-frying at home can be tricky, but this is a very straightforward recipe that provides superb results.

There are two ways to cook these clams: the first, my personal favorite, is by dipping them into a light batter made with egg, milk, and corn flour (a very finely ground cornmeal) and then lightly dredging them in seasoned bread crumbs before deep-frying. This produces clams with a crusty, crunchy exterior. The second is to dip the clams only in the batter before frying, which produces a lighter, less bready exterior that puffs up a bit and creates a more delicate clam.

Dip these tasty morsels in tartar sauce or spicy mayonnaise (page 171). You can also use this recipe for frying oysters, but you need only fry them for a total of 1 minute.

About 4 cups Crisco or vegetable oil
1 large egg
½ cup milk
Dash of Tabasco
Salt
Freshly ground black pepper
¾ cup corn flour (see Note)
1 cup seasoned bread crumbs (optional)
1 pound fresh soft-shell clams, shucked
1 lemon, cut into wedges
Tartar sauce (page 172)

In a large, heavy-bottomed skillet, deep fryer, or wok, heat the Crisco or oil over a moderately high heat until it reaches a temperature of 350 degrees on a deep-frying thermometer.

To make the batter, whisk together the egg, milk, Tabasco, salt, and pepper. Stir in the corn flour and mix to create a somewhat thick batter.

Place the bread crumbs on a large plate.

Dip the clams into the batter for a minute or two. Remove, using chopsticks or a slotted spoon, and very lightly dredge in the bread crumbs, if desired. Place the clams, about 6 at a time, in the hot oil and fry for 2 minutes, turning the clam over after 1 minute. Drain on paper towels and serve immediately with lemon wedges and tartar sauce.

NOTE: Corn flour is very finely ground cornmeal. A fine cornmeal can be substituted. Corn flour is available at health and specialty foods stores.

Linguine with Clam Sauce

SERVES 4

Tender littleneck clams are cooked in the shell with lots of garlic, parsley, and white wine and served over linguine.

1 pound linguine
2 tablespoons olive oil
3 to 4 cloves garlic, finely chopped
2 dozen littleneck clams, scrubbed clean
1 cup finely chopped fresh parsley
Freshly ground black pepper
½ cup dry white wine

Bring a large pot of lightly salted water to boil. Add the linguine and cook for 6 to 8 minutes, or until just tender, or *al dente*. Drain the pasta in a colander; place on a large serving platter and toss with 1 tablespoon of the oil.

While the water is boiling, heat the remaining tablespoon of oil over moderate heat in a large skillet. Add half the garlic and cook for 30 seconds, stirring to prevent the garlic from burning. Add the clams in a single layer if possible, sprinkle the remaining garlic, half the parsley, pepper, and the wine on top and stir well to thoroughly coat the clams. Cover the pan and let cook about 6 minutes, or *just* until the clam shells open. If you let the clams open too wide they will overcook and become tough. Pour the hot clams and sauce over the linguine and sprinkle the remaining parsley on top.

Penne with Grilled Shrimp

SERVES 4

If you make the fra diavolo sauce ahead of time (or use a good bottled marinara and spike it with a touch of cayenne) this dish can be put together in about 20 minutes.

> 1 pound medium-size shrimp (about 30 shrimp),
>   unshelled
> 3 tablespoons good quality olive oil
> Salt
> Freshly ground black pepper
> 2 tablespoons chopped fresh rosemary, or 2 teaspoons
>   dried
> 3 to 3½ cups fra diavolo sauce (page 176)
> One 16-ounce package penne
> 4 tablespoons fresh basil, torn into 1-inch pieces

Place the shrimp in a flat, shallow roasting pan or baking sheet. Brush the oil all over the shrimp and season both sides with salt, pepper, and the rosemary. Let marinate for at least 15 minutes, and up to 24 hours.

Place the fra diavolo sauce in a medium saucepan or skillet and heat about 5 minutes over moderately low heat.

Preheat the broiler or a grill. Bring a large pot of water to a boil, adding a generous pinch of salt. Cook the penne about 8 minutes, or until just tender.

Broil or grill the shrimp about 3 minutes on each side, until cooked through. You can peel the shrimp or serve them with the shells on.

Drain the penne and place in a large bowl. Toss with the fra diavolo sauce. Divide the penne among 4 bowls and top with the shrimp. Sprinkle with the basil.

Shrimp Jambalaya

SERVES 4 GENEROUS PORTIONS

This Louisiana-style stew, made with shrimp, bits of smoky bacon, onions, red and green peppers in a spicy broth, is served over a bed of rice with lime wedges and scallions.

4 strips thick smoked country-style bacon

1½ tablespoons olive oil

1 cup chopped onion

1 red pepper, chopped or thinly sliced

1 green pepper, chopped or thinly sliced

3 stalks celery, chopped

2 whole cloves garlic, plus 4 cloves, chopped

3 scallions, chopped (white and green parts)

2 cups chopped ripe tomatoes, or 2 cups canned
      whole tomatoes with juice

Cayenne pepper to taste

2 tablespoons Cajun spice mixture (see Note)

4 tablespoons flour

1 bay leaf

2 tablespoons chopped fresh thyme, or 2 teaspoons
      dried

4 cups chicken broth, homemade or canned (low-
      sodium variety)

1½ pounds medium-size shrimp, peeled or unpeeled
      (about 35 to 45 shrimp)

2 cups uncooked white rice

Salt

Freshly ground black pepper

1 lime, cut into wedges, for garnish

2 scallions, thinly sliced on the diagonal, for garnish

In a large skillet, cook the bacon over moderate heat until crisp.

In a large soup pot, heat the olive oil over moderate heat. Add the onion and sauté 5 minutes, stirring frequently. Add the peppers, celery, whole and chopped garlic, and scallions and cook another 3 minutes. Add the tomatoes, a pinch of cayenne, and the Cajun spice. Raise the heat and sprinkle the flour on top of the vegetables. Cook for 2 to 3 minutes, or until the roux turns a dark (but not burned) color. Stir in the bay leaf, thyme, and chicken broth and reduce the heat to a gentle simmer.

Meanwhile, remove the cooked bacon from the pan, and drain on a paper towel. Crumble the bacon into 1-inch pieces, and reserve. Drain away all but 1 tablespoon of the bacon fat and place the skillet over a moderately high heat. Add the shrimp and sear on both sides for about 2 minutes. Add the seared shrimp to the pot and cook another 15 minutes.

Make the rice: In a medium saucepan, mix the rice with 4 cups water and a pinch of salt and bring to a boil. Stir the rice, reduce the heat to low, and let cook, covered, until all the water is absorbed and the rice is cooked. Keep warm over a very low heat.

Taste the jambalaya for seasoning; make the stew spicier by adding more cayenne pepper. Add the reserved bacon and heat through. Serve the jambalaya piping hot over a bed of rice, accompanied by the lime wedges and scallions.

NOTE: Cajun spice mixtures are available in specialty food shops and health food stores.

Shrimp Scampi

SERVES 4

Serve these shrimp with rice, over pasta, or with a hunk of warm, crispy French bread to sop up the garlicky juices.

2 tablespoons olive oil

5 to 6 cloves garlic, minced

1 pound medium-size shrimp (25 to 35 shrimp), shelled, with tail intact

¼ cup fish stock or clam juice

2 tablespoons dry white wine

Freshly ground black pepper

3 tablespoons bread crumbs, fresh or dry

2 tablespoons butter, cut into small cubes

1 lemon, cut into wedges

143

Preheat the broiler.

In a large, ovenproof skillet or gratin dish, heat the oil over high heat. Add half the garlic and sauté for 10 seconds. Add the shrimp in one layer and scatter the remaining garlic on top; sear the shrimp for 45 seconds without moving them around at all. Carefully flip the shrimp over and add the stock, wine, and pepper and cook another 45 seconds. Remove the pan from the heat and sprinkle on the bread crumbs; top with the butter cubes. Broil 1 to 2 minutes, or until the bread crumbs turn a golden brown. Serve with the lemon wedges.

Broiled Fish

SERVES 4

The old Lundy's menus always featured broiled fish—generally offering a choice of over ten varieties, ranging from bluefish and cod to sea bass and mackerel. This recipe demands fresh fish.

> 1½ tablespoons butter, cut into small cubes
> 2 pounds fish fillet: bluefish, mackerel, haddock, sole,
>   sea bass, halibut, or any fresh fillet
> Salt
> Freshly ground black pepper
> Sweet paprika
> About ½ cup oreganata mix (page 173)
> 1 lemon, cut into wedges

Preheat the broiler. Grease the bottom of a broiler pan, small shallow roasting pan, or ovenproof skillet with ½ tablespoon of the butter. Add the fish and top with the remaining butter cubes. Season with a touch of salt, pepper, and paprika. Broil for 5 to 8 minutes, depending on the thickness of the fillet. Sprinkle on the oreganata mixture and broil another 1 to 2 minutes, making sure the bread crumbs don't burn. Surround the fish with the lemon wedges.

Pan-Fried Flounder with Brown Butter and Almonds

SERVES 4

You can substitute sole or any other mild-flavored flat fish fillet in this dish. There are several variations to the recipe listed below.

1 cup flour
Salt
Coarsely ground black pepper
2 pounds fillet of flounder or sole
About 1 to 1½ tablespoons vegetable or olive oil
2½ tablespoons butter
½ cup slivered almonds
1 lemon, cut into wedges

145

Place the flour on a large plate and mix in salt and pepper. Lightly dredge both sides of the fish fillets in the seasoned flour.

In a large skillet, or 2 medium skillets, heat 1 tablespoon of the oil and 1 tablespoon of the butter over moderately high heat. Working in batches, sauté the fillets for about 3 minutes on each side, or until golden brown and cooked through. Keep the fillets warm on a plate or serving platter loosely covered with foil while sautéing the remaining fillets; add additional oil if needed.

Melt the remaining 1½ tablespoons butter in the skillet, add the almonds, and sauté until they just begin to turn golden brown, 2 to 3 minutes. Pour the almonds and butter over the sautéed fish and serve with the lemon wedges.

VARIATIONS

- Flounder Sandwich: Omit the almonds and serve the cooked flounder on a bulky roll or 4-inch slice of French bread with tartar sauce (page 172), lettuce, and a squirt of lemon.

- Substitute lime juice for the lemon juice for an interesting twist.

- Add ¼ cup capers to the skillet along with the almonds.

- Sauté ¼ cup chopped red pepper or roasted red pepper with the almonds for added color and flavor.

- Sauté ¼ cup marinated and chopped sun-dried tomatoes with the almonds.

- Substitute walnuts, pine nuts, or pistachios for the almonds.

146

Baked Bluefish
with Basil, Tomatoes, and Onions

SERVES 4

Bluefish is a particularly oily, flavorful fish that can hold up to other strong tastes. You can easily substitute any other variety of firm fish like snapper, haddock, or striped bass.

1 tablespoon olive oil
2 pounds fresh bluefish fillet
2 cloves garlic, thinly sliced
3 tablespoons fresh basil, thinly sliced
1 medium onion, very thinly sliced
2 ripe tomatoes, thinly sliced

Freshly ground black pepper
¼ cup dry vermouth or white wine
3 tablespoons fresh bread crumbs
1 lemon, cut into wedges

Preheat the oven to 400 degrees.

Rub half the oil on the bottom of a medium-size roasting pan, ovenproof skillet, or baking sheet. Place the fish on top and press the garlic into the flesh of the fish. Top with half the basil, then the onion, remaining basil, and finally the tomatoes. Sprinkle with pepper and half the vermouth. Bake for 10 minutes.

Remove from the oven and sprinkle the top of the fish with the bread crumbs and remaining vermouth and bake another 5 to 10 minutes, depending on the thickness of the fish, or until cooked through. Place under the broiler for about 2 minutes, or until the bread crumbs turn golden brown. Serve with the lemon wedges.

147

Crispy Skin Atlantic Salmon with Horseradish Mashed Potatoes and Balsamic Glaze

SERVES 4 GENEROUS PORTIONS

There are several steps involved in this recipe, but if you get organized and do some prep work, the final dish can be put together in very little time. And believe me, it's well worth the effort. Find a good quality but inexpensive balsamic vinegar for making the sauce.

THE HORSERADISH MASHED POTATOES

3 pounds all-purpose or Yukon Gold potatoes, peeled
and cut into large chunks

Salt

7 tablespoons lightly salted butter

1 to 1¾ cups half and half

2 to 4 tablespoons prepared horseradish, drained but
still moist

¼ cup snipped chives

Salt

Freshly ground black pepper

THE BALSAMIC GLAZE

2 cups balsamic vinegar (see above)

4 tablespoons thinly sliced shallots

2 sprigs fresh thyme, chopped, with stems

2 white or black peppercorns

2 bay leaves

½ cup dry white wine

THE SALMON AND CHIVE GARNISH

1½ teaspoons butter, melted

2 pounds fresh Atlantic salmon fillet, skin left on, or
two 1-pound fillets

Salt

Freshly ground black pepper

4 tablespoons dry white wine

¼ cup chopped fresh chives, for garnish

Prepare the potatoes: Place the potatoes in a large pot and
cover with cold water. Add a generous pinch of salt and bring to a
boil. Simmer for 25 to 35 minutes, or until the potatoes are
tender. Drain and let stand about 2 minutes until slightly dry.

Mash the potatoes and add the butter. (Be careful not to overmash or the potatoes will get gummy.) Add the half and half and the horseradish to taste and blend well. Add the chives and season with salt and pepper. Keep warm over a very low heat.

Prepare the balsamic glaze: Place all the ingredients for the glaze in a medium-size nonreactive saucepan and bring to a boil.

Reduce the heat and cook the glaze over a low simmer for about 35 minutes, or until the liquid is reduced to a syrupy glaze that coats the back of a spoon. Be careful not to reduce the liquid too fast or it will become bitter. Strain the glaze through a small strainer into a small bowl or saucepan. At Lundy's the glaze is kept in a plastic squeeze bottle. (The glaze will keep, covered and refrigerated, for up to a month.)

Prepare the salmon and assemble the dish: Preheat the broiler. Brush the bottom of a baking pan or shallow roasting pan with the butter. Season the salmon on both sides with salt and pepper and place it skin side up in the pan. Pour the wine on top. Broil the fish for 2 to 3 minutes, or until the skin is lightly charred and is crispy.

Reduce the oven temperature to 350 degrees and bake for about 9 minutes, or until the salmon is cooked but there is still a touch of pink in the middle.

Place a generous portion of mashed potatoes in the center of a dinner plate and about a ½-pound piece of salmon on top. Spoon or squeeze (if using a bottle) the glaze on top and sprinkle with chives and serve hot.

Salmon with Cornmeal Crust and Almond-Caper Butter

SERVES 4

This fillet of salmon is roasted on a bed of fresh dill, coated with a cornmeal crust, and then finished off with an almond and caper butter. Serve with rice, orzo, or roasted potatoes.

> 1 tablespoon plus 1 teaspoon olive oil
> 1 cup fresh dill, plus 1 tablespoon finely chopped
> 1½ pounds salmon fillet
> Freshly ground black pepper
> 2½ tablespoons fresh lemon juice
> 4 tablespoons coarse cornmeal
> 1 tablespoon butter
> 1 cup slivered almonds
> ¼ cup capers
> 1 lemon, cut into wedges

Preheat the oven to 400 degrees. Grease a shallow roasting pan, ovenproof skillet, or baking dish with 1 tablespoon of the oil. Lay the 1 cup dill in the middle of the pan and place the salmon on top. Grind some pepper on top and pour the lemon juice over the salmon. Roast for 10 minutes. Sprinkle the salmon with cornmeal and roast another 10 minutes.

Meanwhile in a small skillet, heat the butter and remaining teaspoon of oil over moderate heat. Add the almonds and sauté about 4 minutes, or until they just begin to turn golden brown. Add the capers and remove from the heat. Pour the almond-caper butter over the fish and roast another 5 minutes, or until the salmon is cooked through and the sauce is bubbling hot. Surround with the lemon wedges.

Fennel-and-Pepper-Crusted Tuna with Spinach and Orange-Campari Butter Sauce

SERVES 4

Don't be misled by the sophisticated-sounding name of this dish. Almost everything can be prepared ahead of time and the tuna cooked at the very last minute, which makes this an ideal dish for a dinner party.

Fresh tuna steaks are coated in an aromatic mixture of crushed fennel, pepper, cumin, and coriander seeds and sautéed until medium-rare. It is then served over a bed of spinach with a spectacular sauce made from Campari, fresh orange juice, shallots, and white wine. Serve with orzo, rice, or potatoes.

THE FENNEL-PEPPER CRUST
2 tablespoons whole white peppercorns
2 tablespoons fennel seeds
1 tablespoon cumin seeds
1 tablespoon coriander seeds
1 bay leaf, crumbled

THE ORANGE-CAMPARI BUTTER SAUCE
½ cup dry white wine
½ cup orange juice, preferably fresh-squeezed
¼ cup Campari
¼ cup finely minced shallots
½ teaspoon grated orange zest
1 stick (4 ounces) unsalted butter, cut into small
    cubes
Salt
Freshly ground black pepper

151

THE SPINACH

1 tablespoon olive oil

1 pound fresh spinach, stemmed,
   well washed and dried

Salt

Freshly ground black pepper

THE TUNA AND ORANGE GARNISH

1 egg white

Salt

1½ to 2 pounds very fresh tuna steaks, cut about
   ¾ to 1 inch thick, preferably yellowfin

1½ tablespoons olive oil

1 orange, peeled and cut into sections with seeds and
   pith removed

Prepare the fennel-pepper crust: Preheat the oven to 350 degrees. Place all the ingredients in a small, ovenproof skillet and roast for 5 to 8 minutes, or until they just start to brown and you can smell their aroma. Remove from the oven and place in a spice grinder or use a mortar and pestle and grind the mixture until medium-fine. The spices shouldn't be whole, but you don't want them finely ground. (The spices can be prepared at least 24 hours ahead of time. Cover and set aside.)

Prepare the butter sauce: In a nonreactive saucepan, combine the wine, orange juice, Campari, shallots, and orange zest and bring to a boil over high heat. Reduce the heat to medium-high and let simmer for about 15 minutes, until the sauce is syrupy and greatly reduced. Reduce the heat to low and slowly whisk in the butter, a few cubes at a time, whisking constantly to create a smooth sauce. Season with salt and pepper. (The sauce can be covered and refrigerated and kept for 24 hours.)

Prepare the spinach: Place a large skillet over high heat. Add the oil and then the spinach and sauté, stirring constantly, for about 3 minutes, or until just wilted. Drain off any excess liquid and season with salt and pepper. (The spinach can be prepared several hours ahead of time. Cover and refrigerate until ready to use.)

Prepare the tuna and assemble the dish: Place the prepared spice mixture on a large plate. Place the egg white in a bowl and whisk with a fork to loosen it up. Lightly sprinkle the tuna with salt and then brush the egg white on both sides. Sprinkle the toasted spice mixture on *all* sides of the tuna; don't pack it on but sprinkle it to coat.

Heat the sauce over low heat. Heat the spinach over low heat.

Heat a large skillet over high heat. Add the olive oil and let it get hot for a few seconds. Add the tuna and sauté 2 minutes on each side for medium-rare and 1½ minutes per side for rare; the tuna will be thoroughly cooked on the outside and quite pink inside. Remove the tuna and cut it on the diagonal into 4 or 8 pieces. Add the orange sections to the hot pan and let them warm for a minute while you assemble the plates.

Divide the spinach into four portions and place a portion in the center of each plate. Place the tuna on top, balancing it on its side to show off the pink interior of the steak. Spoon the sauce around the plate and add a few orange sections.

Whole Roasted Fish with Potatoes, Fennel, and Shallots

SERVES 4

Try and find a freshly caught whole snapper, flounder, or pompano for this excellent dish. The dish is a whole meal in a dish and takes under 30 minutes to prepare.

4 medium potatoes (Yukon Gold or favorite baking
potato), peeled and quartered
2 large sprigs fresh rosemary
2 whole red snapper, flounder, or pompano
(about 1½ to 1¾ pounds each), cleaned and
gutted, with the head on or off
Salt
Freshly ground black pepper
1 large fennel bulb, or 2 small
4 tablespoons olive oil
4 medium-size shallots, peeled
3 tablespoons fresh lemon juice
1 lemon, cut into 4 wedges, for garnish

Preheat the oven to 450 degrees.

Bring a medium-size saucepan of water to a boil over high heat. Add the potatoes and parboil for 5 minutes. Drain and rinse under cold water to stop the cooking. Drain again, and set aside.

Place a sprig of rosemary in the cavity of each fish and season with salt and pepper. Make three shallow diagonal slits in the skin of the fish.

Cut the fennel lengthwise into thin slices, keeping some of the core to hold the slices together.

Place 1 tablespoon of the oil in a large skillet or shallow roasting pan (large enough to hold both fish and the surrounding vegetables, or drizzle ½ tablespoon oil into 2 medium-size pans—one filled with the fish, the other with the vegetables) and place in the hot oven for 1 to 2 minutes, or until almost smoking. Carefully remove the pan from the oven and place the fish in the middle (be careful of hot, splattering oil) and surround the fish with the parboiled potatoes, fennel slices, and shallots. Drizzle the fish and vegetables with 1 tablespoon of the oil and swirl the pan to coat everything. Season the potatoes and vegetables with salt and pepper. Roast the fish and vegetables for 20 to 30 minutes, depending on the thickness of the fish. There should be no translucency in the fish and it should feel firm at the thickest point.

Remove the fish and vegetables from the oven and drizzle with the remaining 2 tablespoons oil and the lemon juice. Serve sizzling hot accompanied by the lemon wedges.

Roasted Fish Mediterranean Style

SERVES 4

A whole fish (or fillet) is roasted with the flavors of the Mediter-ranean—olive oil, capers, black olives, garlic, tomatoes, and basil. If you like, creamy feta cheese can be sprinkled on top and cooked until it just begins to melt. Serve with a cold, crisp, dry white wine.

4 potatoes, cut into quarters
4 tablespoons olive oil
2 tablespoons chopped fresh oregano or rosemary

Pinch crushed red pepper

Salt

Freshly ground black pepper

2 whole fish (about 1½ to 1¾ pounds each), preferably
    red snapper, striped bass, flounder, pompano, or
    bluefish, scaled and gutted, or a 1-pound fillet

½ cup diced red onions

½ cup pitted black olives

1 cup chopped ripe tomatoes

1 cup chopped ripe yellow tomatoes

2 tablespoons chopped garlic

4 tablespoons fresh basil, cut into thin slices

½ cup dry white wine

½ cup crumbled feta cheese (optional)

1 lemon, cut into wedges

Preheat the oven to 400 degrees.

Place the potatoes in a shallow roasting pan or baking sheet large enough to hold both the fish and potatoes without touching. Add 1 tablespoon of the olive oil, the oregano, crushed red pepper, salt, and pepper; toss to coat. Roast the potatoes for 10 minutes.

Meanwhile, rub 1 tablespoon of oil over the fish and season with salt and pepper. Remove the hot pan from the oven and place the fish in the center surrounded by the preroasted potatoes. Scatter the onions, olives, tomatoes, garlic, and basil on top and around the fish and pour the wine and remaining 2 tablespoons olive oil over the top of each fish. Roast for 20 to 25 minutes, or until the fish is cooked through, depending on the thickness of the fish. Baste the fish once or twice with the pan juices. There should be no translucency in the fish and it should feel firm at the thickest point. Scatter the feta cheese on top of the fish, if desired, and roast another minute or until the cheese just begins to melt. Accompany with the lemon wedges.

10

Poultry and Meat

Lundy's Roasted Marinated Lemon-Herb Chicken

Lundy's Chopped Steak

Grilled New York Strip Steak with Red Wine–Shallot Butter

Broiled Lamb Chops

Lundy's Roasted Marinated Lemon-Herb Chicken

SERVES 4

Marinate the chicken for at least an hour, or preferably overnight, so the lemon, rosemary, thyme, and onion flavors truly permeate the dish.

> One 4-pound chicken, backbone removed and cut
>   into quarters
> 3 tablespoons chopped fresh thyme
> 3 tablespoons chopped fresh rosemary
> 3 scallions, white and green part, finely chopped
> 3 cloves garlic, minced
> 2 tablespoons olive oil
> Salt
> Freshly ground black pepper
> 2 lemons

In a shallow roasting pan, combine the chicken with the thyme, rosemary, scallions, garlic, olive oil, salt, and pepper. Squeeze the juice from the lemons over the chicken and add the shells to the pan. Toss well to coat. Let marinate for 1 to 24 hours.

Preheat the oven to 475 degrees. Remove the lemon shells and roast the chicken skin side up for 20 minutes. Place under the broiler for 5 minutes to crisp up and brown the skin. Serve, topped with the juices.

Lundy's Chopped Steak

SERVES 2 GENEROUS PORTIONS

Whether you call it a hamburger or a chopped steak, this dish has been a treasured item on the Lundy's menu for years. When you order a Lundy's chopped steak you get a large (12-ounce), perfectly broiled burger (it looks more like a Salisbury steak or mini meat loaf) bathed in a rich wine sauce. The sauce served at the restaurant is a bit complex, reducing 4 cups of homemade veal stock with red wine. This simplified version uses canned or homemade stock reduced with red wine and a touch of butter and is well worth your time.

> 2 cups canned or homemade beef or veal stock
> 1 cup dry red wine
> Salt
> Freshly ground black pepper
> 1 tablespoon minced garlic
> 1 pound ground beef, preferably sirloin
> 1 tablespoon butter

Place the stock in a medium saucepan and reduce over high or moderately high heat for about 30 minutes, or until reduced to ½ cup.

Place the wine in another medium saucepan and reduce over high or moderately high heat for about 20 minutes, or until it is reduced to about 2 tablespoons and is the consistency of syrup.

Add the reduced stock to the reduced wine, along with salt, pepper, and the garlic and simmer over moderately high heat for another 5 minutes. (The recipe can be made several hours ahead of time up to this point.)

Preheat the broiler. Form the ground beef into 2 large burgers (the shape of a small meat loaf) and season with salt and pepper. Sprinkle the bottom of an ovenproof medium-size skillet with salt. Place the burgers in the skillet and broil for 10 to 12 minutes for medium-rare. Do not flip the burgers; you want them to obtain a good crust on top.

Remove the burgers from the broiler and transfer to two serving plates and cover loosely with tin foil to keep them warm. Add the reduced sauce to the hot skillet and deglaze the pan. Place over moderate heat and add the butter; let simmer 3 to 5 minutes, or until the butter is melted and the sauce is smooth. Season to taste. Spoon the sauce over the burgers and serve immediately.

Grilled New York Strip Steak with Red Wine—Shallot Butter

SERVES 4

A good grilled steak was always a favorite at Lundy's and this simple recipe is sure to become a winner at your table. The red wine—shallot butter can be made ahead of time and kept in the refrigerator or freezer until ready to use.

THE RED WINE—SHALLOT BUTTER
¼ cup minced shallots
½ tablespoon minced thyme
1 cup dry red wine
¼ pound unsalted butter (1 stick), at room
   temperature

Salt
Freshly ground black pepper

THE STEAKS
Two 16-ounce boneless New York strip steaks, cut
     about 1¼ inches thick
Salt
Freshly ground black pepper
Bunch fresh watercress

Prepare the butter: Combine the shallots, thyme, and wine in a saucepan and bring to a boil. Reduce the heat and let simmer rapidly for about 15 to 20 minutes, or until syrupy. Let cool.

Place the butter in a bowl and mix in the cooled shallot syrup. Place the butter on a piece of waxed paper and shape it into a cylinder with the diameter of a half-dollar. Refrigerate for at least 30 minutes, or freeze for up to 2 weeks.

Prepare the steaks: Preheat the broiler or grill. Season both sides of the steaks with salt and pepper and place on a rack or grilling pan. Broil the meat for 6 to 8 minutes on each side, depending on how rare you like it. Remove from the heat and top each portion with a slice of the butter. Garnish with the watercress.

161

Broiled Lamb Chops

SERVES 4

This simple classic was a popular item on the old Lundy's menu; serve with mint jelly and roasted potatoes.

8 loin-cut lamb chops, cut about 1 inch thick (about 2
    pounds)
1½ tablespoons olive oil
Coarsely ground black pepper
2 tablespoons minced fresh rosemary
Salt
Mint jelly

Place the chops in a large broiler pan or ovenproof skillet and rub the oil, pepper, and rosemary on both sides. Let marinate at room temperature for 15 minutes, or cover and refrigerate and let sit for up to 12 hours.

Preheat the broiler.

Place the chops about an inch away from the broiler and broil for about 4 minutes on each side, or until cooked to medium and pink inside. Sprinkle with salt. Serve with mint jelly.

11

Side Dishes

Lundy's Ultimate Biscuits

Hash Brown Potatoes

Mashed Potatoes with Roasted Garlic

Creamed Spinach

Cole Slaw

Buttermilk Onion Rings

Lundy's Ultimate Biscuits

MAKES ABOUT 14 BISCUITS

After much experimentation, I have gotten this as close to the definitive Lundy's biscuit as you can get. These are light and fluffy biscuits, with a crispy, almost crunchy exterior. Plan on serving the biscuits within a few hours and plan on making a lot—they tend to disappear very quickly. Serve with any of the recipes in this book, or with butter and jam and honey.

> 1½ cups plus 3 tablespoons all-purpose flour
> 1 tablespoon baking powder
> 1 tablespoon sugar
> ½ teaspoon salt
> 4 tablespoons unsalted butter
> 4 tablespoons shortening
> ½ cup milk

Preheat the oven to 375 degrees.

Sift the flour, baking powder, sugar, and salt into a large bowl. Stir well. Cut the butter and shortening into small pieces and add to the flour mixture. Using your hands or a pastry blender, crumble the fat into the flour mixture until the butter and shortening are pea-sized pieces and the mixture resembles coarse cornmeal. Add the milk and mix the dough *just* until it comes together; be careful not to overmix.

Knead the dough gently on a lightly floured work surface. Roll out the dough ½ inch thick; this is a crucial step in making successful biscuits. If you roll the dough out too thin, the biscuits will be dry and overcooked. If you roll it out too thick, they won't cook properly. Using a 2-inch biscuit cutter, or a 2-inch-wide glass, cut out the biscuits and place on an ungreased baking sheet. Roll out the scraps ½ inch thick and cut any additional biscuits. Bake for 14 to 15 minutes, or until the biscuits are golden brown. Serve hot.

Hash Brown Potatoes

SERVES 4

Serve these crisp potatoes with any seafood dish. They make a particularly good brunch accompaniment to the lobster eggs Benedict on page 134. If you use leftover cooked potatoes, the dish can be put together quickly.

1 tablespoon olive oil, or ½ tablespoon oil and ½
    tablespoon butter
1 medium onion, chopped
4 cooked medium potatoes (boiled or roasted), cut
    into slices
1 tablespoon chopped fresh thyme, or 1 teaspoon dried
Salt
Freshly ground black pepper
Sweet paprika

Heat the oil in a large skillet over moderate heat. Sauté the onion for about 6 minutes, stirring frequently, or until soft and golden but not brown. Add the potatoes, thyme, salt, and pepper and let cook another 10 minutes until the potatoes are brown and slightly crisp. Raise the heat to high during the last minute of cooking to really brown and crisp up the potatoes. Sprinkle lightly with paprika and serve hot.

Mashed Potatoes with Roasted Garlic

SERVES 4 GENEROUS PORTIONS

Whole roasted cloves of garlic add a rich dimension and smoky flavor to these creamy potatoes.

  3½ pounds medium all-purpose potatoes, peeled and
      cut into large chunks
  4 tablespoons olive oil
  12 cloves garlic, peeled
  1½ cups low-fat or whole milk
  ⅓ cup heavy cream
  3 tablespoons butter
  Salt
  Freshly ground black pepper

Bring a large pot of lightly salted water to a boil over high heat. Add the potatoes and simmer for about 20 minutes, or until thoroughly tender.

Meanwhile, preheat the oven to 350 degrees.

Place the olive oil in a small, ovenproof skillet or small roasting pan and add the garlic, tossing to coat the cloves. Roast about 7 minutes, or until the cloves are a light golden brown and tender. Remove from the oven and set aside.

Drain the potatoes and reserve ¼ cup of the potato liquid. Place the milk and cream in a saucepan and scald over moderate heat. Mash the potatoes well and add the butter, garlic and oil, and reserved potato water. Add the scalded milk and cream and mash until smooth (or somewhat smooth). Season to taste.

Creamed Spinach

SERVES 4 GENEROUS PORTIONS

Regular creamed spinach can be bland and tasteless, but in this recipe the spinach is sautéed until wilted and then mixed with reduced cream seasoned with nutmeg. The result is a creamy, soothing dish full of the fresh flavor of spinach.

> 3 tablespoons olive oil or butter
> 3 pounds fresh spinach, stemmed, well washed, and
> dried
> 1½ cups heavy cream
> Salt
> Freshly ground black pepper
> About ½ teaspoon freshly ground nutmeg

Place a large skillet over high heat. Add 1 tablespoon of the oil and heat for 10 seconds. Add a pound of spinach and cook for 1 to 2 minutes, or until wilted. Remove and place in a bowl. Repeat with the remaining oil and spinach.

In a large skillet, heat the cream over high heat and reduce until the cream is thick enough to coat the back of a spoon, about 8 minutes. Season with the salt and pepper and nutmeg to taste.

Using your hands, squeeze out any excess moisture from the spinach and chop finely. Add the chopped spinach to the reduced cream and cook over a low heat until the cream is incorporated into the spinach. Check the seasoning and serve hot.

Cole Slaw

SERVES 4

Creamy, sweet, and tart, this cole slaw makes a fine accompaniment to baked, broiled, or fried seafood.

¼ cup mayonnaise

2 tablespoons heavy cream

1 tablespoon sugar

¼ cup chopped onions or scallions (white and green
    parts)

1 tablespoon cider vinegar

2 cups thinly sliced or julienned cabbage, white or
    red, or a combination

1 medium carrot, grated

Salt

Freshly ground black pepper

In a medium bowl, mix the mayonnaise, cream, sugar, onions, and vinegar. Gently stir in the cabbage and carrot and season to taste.

Buttermilk Onion Rings

SERVES 4 GENEROUS PORTIONS

Be careful when you prepare these onion rings because they are highly addictive. Serve as a side dish, a first course, or as a topping for sautéed or grilled fish. Serve with ketchup or hot pepper sauce.

2 large Spanish onions, peeled and sliced into ½-inch-
    thick rounds
2 cups buttermilk
1 teaspoon cayenne
1 teaspoon Tabasco or hot pepper sauce
1 teaspoon Worcestershire sauce
About 1½ cups all-purpose flour
Salt
Freshly ground black pepper
About 4 cups canola or vegetable oil or Crisco

Separate the onions into individual rings and set aside.

In a medium bowl, combine the buttermilk, cayenne, Tabasco, Worcestershire, salt, and pepper. Add the onion rings to the buttermilk mixture and let them marinate for 10 minutes.

Place the flour on a large plate and season liberally with salt and pepper.

Remove the onion rings from the batter and lightly dredge them in the flour. Place on a cookie sheet and set aside.

Heat the oil in a large, heavy-bottomed skillet over moderately high heat until it reaches a temperature of 340 degrees. (If you don't have a thermometer, test the oil by dropping a tiny bit of buttermilk batter in the hot oil; it should sizzle quickly.) Fry the onion rings, working in batches, about 1 to 1½ minutes on each side, or until golden brown. Drain on paper towels, sprinkle lightly with salt, and serve immediately.

12

Sauces and Mixes

Mignonette Sauce

Spicy Mayonnaise

Tartar Sauce

Lundy's Cocktail Sauce

Oreganata Mix

Court Bouillon

Marinara Sauce

Fra Diavolo Sauce

Mignonette Sauce

MAKES ABOUT ½ CUP

Serve with raw oysters. The sauce can be made several hours before serving.

1½ tablespoons coarsely cracked or crushed black
    peppercorns
2 tablespoons minced shallots
¼ cup red wine vinegar
¼ cup good quality cider vinegar

Combine all the ingredients in a small bowl and serve.

Spicy Mayonnaise

MAKES ½ CUP

This simple, delightfully spicy dipping sauce is ideal for the fried seafood fritters or any fried or broiled seafood dish. Try it with fried clams. The sauce can be made several hours before serving.

½ cup homemade or commercial mayonnaise
1 teaspoon Worcestershire sauce
½ to 1 teaspoon Tabasco or hot pepper sauce
1½ teaspoons fresh lemon juice
About ½ teaspoon sweet paprika or cayenne pepper

In a medium bowl, mix the mayonnaise, Worcestershire, Tabasco, and lemon juice. Taste for seasoning and add more

Tabasco if you like. Sprinkle on enough paprika or cayenne to taste; the paprika will give the sauce a sweet flavor and the cayenne will give it a spicy bite. Keep cold and serve.

Tartar Sauce

MAKES ABOUT 2 CUPS

The classic accompaniment to fried seafood. Tartar sauce can be made several hours before serving.

⅛ cup capers
⅛ cup chopped parsley
⅛ cup chopped cornichons or gherkins
1½ cups mayonnaise
¼ cup diced onions
⅛ cup lemon juice
⅛ teaspoon Dijon mustard
Dash of Tabasco or hot pepper sauce
Salt
Freshly ground black pepper

Place the capers, parsley, and cornichons in the container of a food processor and pulse until finely chopped. (Alternately, finely chop the ingredients by hand.) Place in a medium bowl and mix in the mayonnaise, onions, lemon juice, mustard, hot pepper sauce, salt, and pepper. Cover and refrigerate until ready to use.

Lundy's Cocktail Sauce

MAKES ABOUT 1 CUP

The classic accompaniment to shrimp cocktail. The sauce will keep for several hours before serving.

½ cup ketchup
½ cup chili sauce
1½ to 2 tablespoons horseradish, drained
2 tablespoons lemon juice
2 tablespoons minced parsley
½ teaspoon Tabasco or hot pepper sauce
1 tablespoon Worcestershire sauce

In a medium bowl, mix all the ingredients. Taste and adjust the horseradish and Tabasco if you like a spicier sauce.

Oreganata Mix

MAKES ABOUT 1 CUP

This savory mixture is used to stuff clams and lobsters at Lundy's. You could also use it to stuff shrimp or mussels, or simply sprinkle it on top of a fillet or fish steak and broil until golden brown. The mixture will keep, covered and refrigerated, for up to a week.

1 tablespoon olive oil
2 tablespoons minced garlic
½ cup dry bread crumbs

½ cup fresh bread crumbs (see Note)
2 tablespoons dried oregano
3½ tablespoons minced parsley
3 tablespoons melted butter
2½ tablespoons fresh lemon juice

In a small skillet, heat the oil over moderate heat. Sauté the garlic for 1 to 2 minutes, or until just softened and a light golden color; be careful not to let it brown.

Transfer the garlic and oil to a small bowl and add the remaining ingredients and toss well. Keep covered and refrigerate until ready to use.

NOTE: Place a small hunk of crusty, slightly stale bread in a food processor and process until the bread has the consistency of coarse bread crumbs.

Court Bouillon

MAKES ABOUT 6 CUPS

A light, vegetable-based stock for poaching seafood.

6 cups water
2 onions, peeled and thinly sliced
1 lemon, washed and cut in half
2 carrots, thinly sliced
2 stalks of celery, thinly sliced

2 tablespoons peppercorns
1 tablespoon fresh thyme, or 1 teaspoon dried
3 tablespoons coarsely chopped fresh parsley
1 cup dry white wine
Salt

In a stockpot, combine the water, onions, lemon, carrots, celery, peppercorns, thyme, and parsley and bring to a boil. Simmer for 20 minutes and add the wine and salt. Simmer another 10 to 15 minutes and season to taste. Strain the court bouillon and bring to a simmer for poaching or freeze until ready to use. (The court bouillon can be reused after poaching fish. Strain and bring to a boil and refrigerate or freeze until ready to reuse.)

Marinara Sauce

MAKES ABOUT 4 CUPS

This flavorful marinara sauce can be served over pasta or with shellfish or the penne with grilled shrimp on page 140. Make the sauce ahead of time and cover and refrigerate for several days, or freeze for up to 3 months.

1 tablespoon olive oil
1 medium red onion, finely chopped
1 medium yellow onion, finely chopped
6 cloves garlic, chopped
One 28-ounce can whole tomatoes and juice

One 6-ounce can tomato paste
⅓ cup dry red wine
2 tablespoons balsamic vinegar
¼ cup chopped fresh basil
Salt
Freshly ground black pepper

In a large saucepan, heat the oil over a moderately low heat. Add the onions and half the garlic and sauté for 6 minutes, or until softened but not brown. Stir in the whole tomatoes, breaking them up with your hands, along with the juice, tomato paste, red wine, vinegar, basil, salt, pepper, and the remaining garlic and simmer over low heat for about 45 minutes. Season to taste.

FRA DIAVOLO SAUCE

To make a fra diavolo sauce, prepare the marinara sauce and add a pinch of crushed red pepper and a pinch of cayenne pepper to taste during the last 5 minutes of simmering.

13

Desserts

Rice Pudding

Lundy's Chocolate Cake

Lundy's Cheesecake

Blueberry (or Huckleberry) Pie

Rice Pudding

SERVES 6

Infused with the subtle flavors of cinnamon, vanilla, and lemon, this is one of the richest, creamiest rice puddings imaginable. The pudding can be served cold, at room temperature, or with a brûlée-like sugar coating on top.

> 5 cups milk, whole or 2%
> ½ cup rice
> ⅓ cup plus ¼ cup sugar, plus additional for brûlée-style garnish
> ½ cinnamon stick
> 2 thin strips lemon zest
> ½ stick vanilla, or ¼ teaspoon vanilla extract
> Pinch salt
> 1 cup heavy cream
> 1 large egg yolk

In a large, heavy-bottomed pot, combine the milk, rice, ⅓ cup sugar, cinnamon stick, lemon zest, vanilla, and salt; bring to a vigorous simmer. Reduce the heat to low and let simmer for 1 hour, stirring frequently with a wooden spoon or spatula. (If you don't stir frequently a thick layer of milk will form on the top and have to be removed.) Remove from the heat and let the rice cool slightly.

Meanwhile, in a bowl whisk the cream, egg yolk, and ¼ cup sugar. Once the rice is cooled and slightly thick, add a few tablespoons to the bowl of cream. Pour the cream into the pot and continue to cook over a low heat until thick enough to coat the back of a spoon. Remove the cinnamon stick, vanilla stick, and lemon strips and discard. Let cool slightly and transfer to a large ovenproof serving bowl or place in individual ramekins. Cover with waxed paper or plastic wrap and refrigerate for at least 2 hours.

To serve the pudding brûlée-style: Preheat the broiler. Keep the pudding in the ovenproof serving bowl or individual ramekins. Sprinkle 4 to 6 tablespoons of white sugar on top of the bowl or about 1 tablespoon on top of each pudding ramekin and broil for about 2 minutes, or until golden brown and crusty. Remove and serve. The pudding will be cool and the sugar topping should be hard and caramelized.

Lundy's Chocolate Cake

SERVES 10

This rich, moist, six-layer cake with a whipped cream filling and a super creamy cocoa frosting has great appeal. The cake can be assembled several hours before serving.

THE CAKE

1 cup unsweetened cocoa powder
2 cups boiling water
½ pound (2 sticks) unsalted butter
2½ cups sugar
4 eggs
1½ teaspoons vanilla extract
2¾ cups all-purpose flour
2 teaspoons baking soda
½ teaspoon salt
½ teaspoon baking powder

THE CREAM FILLING
1 cup heavy cream
¼ cup confectioners' sugar
1 teaspoon vanilla

THE COCOA FROSTING
½ pound (8 ounces) semisweet chocolate
1 cup heavy cream
6 tablespoons light corn syrup

Prepare the cake: Lightly grease and flour three 10-inch cake pans and set aside.

Preheat the oven to 350 degrees.

In a medium saucepan, combine the cocoa and boiling water, whisking to prevent lumps.

Using a mixer and a large bowl, cream the butter and sugar until soft and smooth. Add the eggs, one at a time, and then the vanilla and beat until smooth.

Sift the flour, baking soda, salt, and baking powder into a bowl. Add the flour mixture alternately with the cocoa mixture and beat until smooth. Divide the batter into the three pans and bake for 25 to 30 minutes; the cake is done when a toothpick inserted in the center of the cake comes out clean. Let the cakes cool and remove them from the pans.

Meanwhile, prepare the cream filling: Beat the cream until peaks form and whip in the confectioners' sugar and vanilla. Cover and refrigerate until ready to use.

Prepare the frosting: In the top of a double boiler set over simmering water, melt the chocolate and cream together until the chocolate is smooth. Add the corn syrup and simmer for 5 minutes, or until very hot.

To assemble the cake, cut each cake in half horizontally using a large, serrated knife. Place one layer of cake on a large cake plate and, using a spatula, smooth some of the whipped cream on it. Place another cake layer on top and spread with cream; repeat with an additional three layers of cake and the remaining whipped cream. Place the last, sixth layer of cake on top of the whipped cream. Pour the hot icing over the top of the cake, letting it spill over the sides. Refrigerate for several hours to set before serving.

Lundy's Cheesecake

SERVES 12

Moist, rich, and creamy, this cheesecake should be baked several hours before serving in order to give it time to chill properly. Serve with strawberries or assorted fresh fruit.

2½ pounds (40 ounces) cream cheese
1 pint sour cream
1½ cups sugar
4 large eggs
3 tablespoons milk
3 tablespoons heavy cream
¼ teaspoon vanilla extract

Preheat the oven to 325 degrees. Grease the bottom and sides of a 10-inch springform pan with a removable bottom. Fill a large roasting pan with about an inch of cold water and set aside.

In a large mixing bowl, whip the cream cheese with an electric beater until softened. Add the sour cream and sugar and beat until light and fluffy. Add the eggs, one at a time, and then the milk, cream, and vanilla and continue beating until light and fluffy. Pour the mixture into the greased pan. Put the pan into the roasting pan with the water and place on the middle shelf of the preheated oven. Bake for 2½ hours, or until golden brown and firm. If the cheesecake appears to be browning too quickly, cover loosely with aluminum foil and bake until firm. While the cheesecake is baking, check the water bath and make sure the water hasn't evaporated; pour additional water *around* the cake if needed.

Remove from the oven and let cool. Unmold the cake and let chill for at least 4 hours.

Blueberry (or Huckleberry) Pie

SERVES 6

Lundy's has long been famous for their homemade fruit pies—blueberry, apple, huckleberry, and more. The traditional Lundy's pie was made in a twelve-inch round aluminum pie plate, looking very much like a toy flying saucer, that customers coveted. When you bought a whole pie from Lundy's you would pay a small deposit on the pan and take the whole thing home with you. The assumption was that the pie plate would eventually make its way back to the restaurant, but for many the pie plate was as much of a treat as the pie.

This blueberry pie has an exceedingly flaky pastry and lots of fresh fruit. Plan on making the pastry at least an hour or two before baking in order to give it time to chill properly before rolling it out. Serve the pie warm or at room temperature with whipped cream or vanilla ice cream.

THE CRUST
2 cups all-purpose flour
Pinch salt
⅔ cup butter, lard, or vegetable shortening, cut into
    small pieces
¼ to ⅓ cup *ice* cold water

THE FILLING
2 pints fresh or frozen blueberries
½ cup sugar
¼ teaspoon vanilla extract
2 tablespoons flour

THE GLAZE
About ¼ cup milk
About 2 tablespoons sugar

To make the crust, sift the flour and salt into a large bowl. Add the butter, lard, or shortening and, using a pastry cutter or two flat knives, work the fat into the flour until the mixture resembles cornmeal. Add the water, beginning with ¼ cup, stirring the liquid in with a fork. Add just enough water so that the dough holds together. Wrap in waxed paper and refrigerate for a minimum of 1 hour and up to 24 hours.

Preheat the oven to 350 degrees. Sprinkle a work surface with flour and roll out a little more than half the dough. Line a 9-inch pie plate with the dough and crimp the edges.

In a large bowl, combine the berries, sugar, vanilla, and flour. Pour the filling into the crust.

Roll out the remaining dough (as well as any scraps remaining from the bottom crust). Lightly brush the edges of the bottom crust with a little water to help seal the crusts, place the top crust over the berry filling, and crimp the edges, if desired. Use a fork to pierce the top of the dough in several spots (this will help release steam as it bakes). Bake for 30 minutes. Remove the pie from the oven and brush the top with milk, using a pastry brush or the back of a spoon. Sprinkle with sugar and bake another 15 to 20 minutes, or until the crust is golden and the berry mixture begins to bubble. Let sit 5 minutes before serving.

14

Drinks

185

The martini menu at Lundy's is extensive, with drinks named for legendary Brooklyn characters and locales, offering a taste for everyone. All martinis serve one.

F.W.I.L.

Named for Irving Lundy, this classic martini features whole shrimp garnish.

3 ounces vodka, preferably Absolut Peppar
1 ounce tomato juice
Dash of Tabasco or hot pepper sauce
2 whole cooked shrimp, peeled and deveined

Mix the vodka, tomato juice, and Tabasco and shake well. Pour into a martini glass and garnish each side of the glass with a shrimp.

The Linker

This fruity martini, with a dash of cranberry and strawberry liqueur, is named in honor of Lundy's business associate and partner, "Uncle" Henry Linker.

3½ ounces vodka
½ ounce strawberry liqueur
Dash of cranberry juice
1 strawberry

Mix the vodka, strawberry liqueur, and cranberry juice and shake well. Pour into a martini glass and garnish with the strawberry.

~~~~~

Irish Setter

A delicious after-dinner martini.

> 1½ to 2 ounces good quality Irish whiskey, preferably Bushmill
> 1½ to 2 ounces green crème de menthe

Mix the whiskey and crème de menthe in a shaker and strain into a martini glass.

~~~~~

The Sound

> 2 to 2½ ounces vodka or Finlandia pineapple vodka
> 2 to 2½ ounces Malibu rum
> Slice of fresh pineapple
> Cherry

Mix the vodka and rum in a shaker and strain into a martini glass. Garnish with the pineapple and cherry.

The Lincoln Zephyr

This drink has a delightful chocolate and banana aftertaste.

3 ounces vodka
¾ ounce crème de cacao
½ ounce crème de banana
Cherry

Shake the vodka, crème de cacao, and crème de banana and strain into a martini glass. Garnish with the cherry.

188

The Madeline

This drink was named for Madeline, the daughter of Frank and Jeanne Cretella, the current owners of Lundy's.

3 ounces vodka
2 ounces chambord
Slice of orange

Shake the vodka and chambord together and strain into a martini glass. Garnish with the orange.

Lundy's Brooklyn Egg Cream

SERVES 1

Egg creams are legendary in Brooklyn. Searching for a recipe for the classic, definitive Brooklyn egg cream is an exercise in frustration. Everyone I interviewed—from chefs and bartenders to Brooklyn housewives and old-timers—offered a different recipe. "You want the real Brooklyn egg cream?" asked a seventy-year-old man from Sheepshead Bay. "Well, I know it, but I'm not going to tell you it for fear it will get into the wrong hands."

"Follow my recipe and you won't taste a better egg cream ever, anywhere, I promise you that," said a woman with teased, fluffy gray hair, sitting at the raw bar at Lundy's early one summer Sunday evening. But my favorite comment was from a Lundy's waiter who whispered in my ear, in a conspiratorial tone: "No one knows the real recipe for egg cream, but I'm a nice guy and I'm gonna give it to you 'cause I like you."

Egg creams never appeared on the old Lundy's menu, but this is the Brooklyn-style egg cream currently being served at Lundy's. This drink is made with Fox's U-Bet chocolate syrup, milk, and seltzer. According to one of the bartenders at Lundy's: "The trick to a good egg cream is to give it a good 'head' and stir the drink in a continuous circular motion." Some of the Brooklynites I spoke with insist that you must drink an egg cream accompanied by a pretzel rod (or stick). Give it a try and you'll instantly be transported to Sheepshead Bay.

2 ounces Fox's U-Bet chocolate syrup (see Note)
2½ ounces milk
Seltzer to taste

Pour the chocolate syrup and milk into a 16-ounce glass. Add the seltzer and stir the drink in a continuous circular motion until there is nice white foam on top. Serve with a straw.

NOTE: For information on ordering Fox's U-Bet syrup, write to:
H. Fox's and Co., Brooklyn, New York 11212,
or call: (718) 385-4600.

Acknowledgments

ROBERT CORNFIELD   I owe special thanks to Carol and Fred Bamert, Allen Lundy, Janet Higgins, and Jeanne and Frank Cretella of the Tam Corporation; also to Adrienne Lowe, Bruce McCurdy, Steve Gattulo, John O'Connell; to Herb Shalat; to Neil Kleinberg, who became a friend, and Ron Schweiger, who was generous and enthusiastic at the most crucial moments; to Brian Merlis, collector extraordinaire; the remarkable and inspiring Margaret McCord; Lois Riss and Marion Anderson; and to Brooklyn historian John Manbeck. Elliot Willensky's contribution is excerpted from his book *When Brooklyn Was the World* (copyright © 1986 by Elliot Willensky), and is used with the kind permission of Crown Publishers, Inc.

I am also grateful for the generous help and consideration given me at the Brooklyn Public Library, by Clara Lamers at the Brooklyn Historical Association, by the New York Historical Society, and by Gale Harris and Marian Cleaver of the Research Department at the Landmarks Preservation Commission. I am also grateful to the staffs of Butler and Avery Libraries at Columbia University; Special Collections at Brooklyn College; the U.S. History, Local History, and Genealogy Division of the New York Public Library; and the Astor, Lenox, and Tilden Foundations. Valiant Sharon Bowers of HarperCollins made it happen, and Georges Borchardt proved to be, as always, as splendid a friend as he is an agent.

KATHY GUNST   I would like to thank Bob Cornfield, friend, agent, and writer, for inviting me to get involved with this project. He reintroduced me to the culinary wonders of Lundy's and spent hours showing me his hometown, Brooklyn, New York. I would never have known its beauty without you, Bob.

Many thanks to my new friend, Chef Neil Kleinberg, for opening his kitchen and recipe files to me. His extraordinary talent, generosity, and humor have made so many of the recipes in this book possible. And thanks to all the other Lundy's cooks and bakers. It was quite an education to spend a week inside the Lundy's kitchen and see the intense work and dedication that goes into producing such delicious food.

And to my family, John, Maya, and Emma, for sharing all this fantastic seafood and gobbling it up so enthusiastically.

192

LUNDY MEMORIES HONOR ROLL   We also want to thank those patrons who contributed their memories:

Bruce Danbrot

Louis Fasano

Edward Hellenbrand

Cliff Lobel

Blanche Madden

Angelo Moronese

Harold Parker

Richard Redley

Mildred Rosenberg

Margaret Scicolone

Annette Stein

Ann Travis

Jerry Wolf

Marvin Zank

Bibliography

In addition to the books listed below, the history of Sheepshead Bay and the early history of the Lundy family is based on newspaper accounts of the *Brooklyn Daily Eagle* in the *Eagle* clippings file of the Brooklyn Public Library at Grand Army Plaza. Additional newspaper clippings concerning the later years from the New York *Daily News*, *The New York Times*, and the New York *Herald Tribune* were made available to me at the Landmarks Preservation Commission.

The American Institute of Architects, Long Island Chapter, and The Society for the Preservation of Long Island Antiquities. *AIA Architectural Guide to Nassau and Suffolk Counties, Long Island*. New York: Dover Publications, Inc., 1992.

Armstrong, William Clinton. *The Lundy Family and Their Descendants*. New Brunswick, N.J.: J. Heidingsfeld, 1902.

Berman, Marshall. *All That Is Solid Melts Into Air: The Experience of Modernity*. New York: Penguin Books, 1988.

Della Femina, Jerry, and Charles Sopkin. *An Italian Grows in Brooklyn*. Boston: Little, Brown & Company, 1978.

Dreiser, Theodore. *The Color of a Great City*. New York: Syracuse University Press, 1996.

Fischler, Stan. *Confessions of a Trolley Dodger from Brooklyn*. Flushing, N.Y.: H&M Productions II Inc., 1995.

Frommer, Myrna Katz, and Harvey Frommer. *It Happened in Brooklyn: An Oral History of Growing Up in the Borough in the 1940s, 1950s, and 1960s*. San Diego, New York, and London: Harcourt Brace & Company, 1993.

Gelernter, David. *1939: The Lost World of the Fair*. New York: The Free Press, 1995.

Ierardi, Eric J. *Gravesend: The Home of Coney Island*. New York: Vantage Press, 1975.

Jackson, Kenneth T., ed. *The Encyclopedia of New York City*. New Haven and London: Yale University Press, 1995.

Koolhas, Rem. *Delirious New York: A Retroactive Manifesto for Manhattan*. New York: The Monacelli Press, 1994.

Landmarks Preservation Commission. "F.W.I.L. Lundy Brothers Restaurant Building." Report prepared by Gale Harris, and edited by Elisa Urbanelli. New York: Landmarks Preservation Commission, 1992.

Lines, Ruth L. "The Story of Sheepshead Bay, Manhattan Beach, and the Sheepshead Bay Library." New York: Brooklyn Public Library, 1949.

McCullough, Edo. *Good Old Coney Island*. New York: Charles Scribner's Sons, 1957

Merlis, Brian. *Brooklyn: The Way It Was*. Brooklyn: Israelowitz Publishing, 1995.

Merlis, Brian, and Oscar Israelowitz, *Welcome Back to Brooklyn*. Brooklyn: Israelowitz Publishing, 1993.

Merlis, Brian, Lee A. Rosenzweig, and I. Stephen Miller. *Brooklyn's Gold Coast: The Sheepshead Bay Communities*. Brooklyn: The Sheepshead Bay Historical Society, in association with Israelowitz Publishing and Brooklyn Editions, 1997.

Milgram, Joseph B. *An Informal History of Sheepshead Bay*. New York: Brooklyn Public Library, 1972.

Monti, Ralph. *I Remember Brooklyn: Memories from Famous Sons and Daughters*. New York: Carol Publishing Group, 1991.

Moore, Deborah Dash. *At Home in America: Second Generation New York Jews*. New York: Columbia University Press, 1981.

O'Neill, Molly. *New York Cookbook*. New York: Workman, 1992.

Orleck, Annelise, and Alexis Jetter. "A Mistrust of Strangers." *The Newsday Magazine*, September 24, 1989:11–15, 18–20.

Pilat, Oliver, and Jo Ransom. *Sodom by the Sea*. New York: Doubleday, Doran Company, 1941.

Prince, Carl E. *Brooklyn's Dodgers: The Bums, the Borough, and the Best of Baseball*. New York and Oxford: Oxford University Press, 1996.

Sanders, Ronald. *Reflections on a Teapot*. New York: Harper & Row Publishers, 1972.

Snyder-Grenier, Ellen M. *Brooklyn! An Illustrated History*. Philadelphia: Temple University Press, 1996.

Stallworth, Lyn, and Rod Kennedy, Jr. *The Brooklyn Cookbook*. New York: Alfred A. Knopf, 1993.

Stern, Robert A. M., Gregory Gilmartin, and Thomas Mellins. *New York 1930. Architecture and Urbanism Between the Two World Wars*. New York: Rizzoli, 1987.

Stiles, Henry R. *History of the County of Kings and the City of Brooklyn, from 1683 to 1884*. New York: W. W. Munsell & Co., 1884.

Weld, Ralph Foster. *Brooklyn Is America*. New York: Columbia University Press, 1950.

Willensky, Elliot. *When Brooklyn Was the World, 1920–1957*. New York: Harmony Books, 1986.

Index

203

Shore Dinner

$5.50

Celery

Clam, Oyster, Shrimp or Crabmeat Cocktail

Steamed Clams with Butter Sauce and Broth

Half Broiled Lobster

Half Broiled Chicken

Julienne Potatoes   Fresh Vegetable

Ice Cream   or   Home Made Pie

Coffee, Tea or Milk

Chicken--Lobster Dinner

$3.25 $3.25

Tomato Juice or

Cup of Clam Broth or Chowder

Broiled Chicken or Cold Lobster

Julienne Potatoes   Fresh Vegetable

Ice Cream   or   Home Made Pie

Coffee, Tea or Milk

Fish Dinner

$2.75

Tomato Juice or

Cup of Clam Broth or Chowder

Choice of Fish

Julienne Potatoes   Fresh Vegetable

Ice Cream   or   Home Made Pie

Coffee, Tea or Milk

We suggest a dry white wine with seafood, such as
CHABLIS - Glass .60 - ½ Bottle $2.75 - Bottle $4.75

A La Carte

RELISHES	Celery ...... .40	Olives ...... .30		Tomato Juice
COCKTAILS	Lobster Cocktail ..1.75	Oyster Cocktail ...... .60		Clam Juice Co
	Shrimp Cocktail ..1.00	Crabmeat Cockt'l 1.00		Clam Cocktail

	Clam Chowder ...... .45	Chicken Soup, Cup	
	Cup ...... .25	Oysters on Half Shell	
	Clam Bisque ...... .45	Oyster Stew	
OYSTERS	Cup ...... .25	Oyster Pan Roast	
and	Clam Broth ...... .45	Clams on Half Shell	
CLAMS	Cup ...... .25	Clam Stew	
	Fish Chowder ...... .45	Soft Clam Pan Roast	
	Cup ...... .25	Steamed Clams	

		Mackerel
	Oysters 1.50	Sea Bass
	Soft Clams 1.50	Sea Scallops
FRIED	Hard Clams 1.50	Shrimps
SEAFOOD	Bluefish 1.50	Smelts
	Filet of Cod 1.50	2 Soft Shell Crabs on
	Filet of Sole 1.50	Tartar

		Sliced Tomatoes
	Lobster 2.25	Hearts of Lettuce
SALADS	Shrimp 1.75	Lettuce and Tomato
	Crabmeat 1.75	
	Cold Boiled Lobster 2.25	

	Lundy's Special Hot BOILED	Filet of Sole
	Lobster, Butter Sauce 3.00	Mackerel
BROILED	Broiled Live Lobster 3.25	Oysters
SEAFOOD	Bluefish 1.50	Sea Bass
	Filet of Cod 1.50	Smelts
	Scallops 1.50	Shrimp

NEWBURGHS	Lobster 2.50	Crabmeat 2.00	Sh
or AU GRATIN			

			Half Broiled Ch
	Club Steak 4.50		Lamb Chops (2)
STEAKS,	Lundy's Special Steak Dinner 5.00		Ham or Bacon a
CHOPS, etc.	Lamb Chop Dinner 3.75		Fresh Long Isla
	Chopped Steak Dinner 3.25		(any style)
	Chopped Steak 2.00		

			Potatoes —
	Corn on Cob ...... .50		Julienne
	Cauliflower ...... .40		French Frie
VEGETABLES	String Beans ...... .40		Lyonnaise
and	Peas ...... .50		Hashed B
POTATOES	Fried Onions ...... .50		Baked
	French Fried Onions ...... .50		Boiled

			Filet of Sole
	Oyster ...... .60		Cheese
SANDWICHES	Clam ...... .60		Ham
	Scallop ...... .60		Egg
	Shrimp ...... .60		

DESSERTS	Home Made Pies ...... .40	Watermelon ...... .40
	Home Made Pies to Take Home	

			Pepsi Co
	Coffee or Tea ...... .15		Ginger
	Iced Coffee ...... .20		Orange
BEVERAGES	Iced Tea ...... .20		Club So
	Milk ...... .15		7 Up
	Coca Cola ...... .15		

COMPLETE WINE LIST IS ON OT

ALE
BATT'S ALE (IMPORTED
WE RESER